W0115554

1,000 Jokes
for Auto Aficionados

PAUL J. PLACEK, PH.D.

Copyright © 2020 by Paul J. Placek, Ph.D.

All rights reserved. No part of this publication may be reproduced, distributed, or transmitted in any form or by any means, including photocopying, recording, or other electronic or mechanical methods, without the prior written permission of the publisher, except in the case of brief quotations embodied in critical reviews and certain other noncommercial uses permitted by copyright law. For permission requests, write to the author, addressed "Attention: Permissions " at PJPLACEK@ VERIZON.NET.

Print ISBN: 978-1-09831-747-8
eBook ISBN: 978-1-09831-748-5

Printed in the United States of America on SFI Certified paper.

First Edition

PREFACE

I was born at a very early age when dinosaurs roamed the earth. Now, at age 74, I confess to still being an auto aficionado*, enthusiast, motor head, and car guy. I have owned over 40 old cars, mostly mid-50s parts and project Fords. I've had so many that I still sell used parts.

NO, THAT'S NOT RIP TAYLOR (COMEDIAN, 1931-2019) THAT'S PAUL PLACEK!

*Aficionado [e,fiSHe'nodo, e,fisye'nado] - A person who is very knowledge-able and enthusiastic about an activity subject, or pastime.

It all began when I was just 10 years old, in 1955, when I mounted a lawnmower engine on my Schwinn bike. When I was 12, I talked my Dad out of the family lawnmower and built a go-cart out of junk. It had no brakes, and the cop who red-lighted me in Midlothian, Illinois pointed that out to my mother after he made me walk it home. A Whizzer motorbike at age 14 followed and then our family moved to Florida, where I got a Vespa at age 15. At 16, I paid $200 for a 1952 Plymouth Cranbrook which was soon rear-ended and nearly totaled by a Greyhound Bus (his fault!). Somewhat drivable, I drove it, and put "DANGER, BLIND MAN DRIVING" on the driver's door. Even though it had an exhaust cut-out and flames, the judge ruled in my favor. On the trunk, I painted 'YOU SHOULD SEE THE OTHER GUY!" Then, at age 16, my Dad helped me buy a 1955 Ford four-door Customline with I-6 and Fordomatic. I was earning 25 cents an hour at our family's A & W Drive-In Restaurant, and with my modest earnings, I paid off the $425 Ford. I put 100,000 miles on it and when I was age 21, I sold it to a bodacious blonde for $140. Many typical things happened in that '55 during my teen years—at the drive-in, girlfriends, informal drag races, driving to another state to buy (and resell) illegal fireworks, going to New Smyrna and Daytona Beach, and going to the demolition derbies. Yes, all that in my '55 Ford. By age 19, my play car was a $75 1937 Ford Coupe which had no engine or tranny. For the drive train I bought a $40 1951 Ford Victoria hard top with a smoky flathead eight and stick shift. Also, I bought a 1946 Opel for $15 to run in a local demolition derby.

However, the toys went away after I finished Junior College and left Sanford, Florida. I attended Florida State University (FSU) in Tallahassee in 1965. After Bachelor's and Master's Degrees from FSU and three years of college teaching in Chattanooga, it was on to Vanderbilt University in Nashville for three years to earn my Ph.D. In Tennessee, I got into mountain four-wheeling with a Jeepster Commando. Then, with a new Federal job in Maryland came a Chevy Tahoe.

In 1984, I got a good tax refund. A 1964 TBird appeared, soon to be followed by a 1965 TBird and a 1946 Chevy. And all of them ran! Then a yellow '64 TBird, a red and black '65 TBird and a black '66 TBird convertible. Again, all ran! A few stayed, most went. But for each one which went away, two more appeared. Over twenty-five 1955-56 Fords slowly appeared, along with garages to keep them in.

WILD AUTHOR WITH HIS CUSTOMIZED '55 FORD

I eventually built an eight-car garage here at my Maryland home of 43 years. I still have a '41 Ford Coupe with a 429 CJ engine, a '49 Hudson with 360 Fury III power, a '55 Ford Sunliner, a '55 Ford Glasstop Crown Victoria, and custom-made golf carts made into '55 and '56 Fords.

REBECCA AND PAUL PLACEK IN 1956 FORD GOLF CART

I also built a three-car garage at a rental house. I also bought a rental house simply because it had two garages! We joined a half-dozen car clubs, and still belong to the Kent Island Cruisers and the Crown Victoria Association. Furthermore, through building all the garages, fixing all the cars, working full-time, and editing car club mags, and writing jokes, I had an excellent partner.

For 42 years, I have had the assistance of the most supportive wife a man could have—my sweet Becky. She typed and proofed innumerable car club newsletters, and proofed statistical and scientific books. More recently, for 15 months, we labored daily on this joke book. This book would not have been published without her tech help and organization skills. I reworked some jokes four times, and she cheerfully dealt with my chicken scratching.

I also appreciate the generosity of George Trosley, a celebrity among those illustrators who do cartoon car art and humor. I have admired him since his "Krass N Bernie" series in CARtoons. He allowed me to use some of his TOOL BOX 'TOONS which matched up well with specific jokes.

I also thank Shelby Rehn, a talented artist who ably interpreted 70 of my jokes and translated them into her illustrations.

Since I was surrounded on all sides by old cars, my friends mistakenly assumed that I must know something about old cars. So 26 years ago, we helped start the Kent Island Cruisers here in Maryland. I was (for ten years) the Editor of Cruiser News. Then 22 years ago, I took the Editor's job for the Crown Victoria Association, which worshipped the 1954-55-56 Ford cars. Into every monthly issue I wrote and inserted car jokes. Twenty-six years with two jokes x 12 months = 600 jokes! Then I added 400 more. Thus, 1,000 jokes!

The jokes came from everywhere—the internet (I rewrote them), joke books (again, rewritten), friends, movies, and real life. I gave each joke a new title. I ran every joke in this book through a plagiarism program twice (ProWritingAid), and if five or more words were the same as some other joke in the computer world, I rewrote it totally or cited it.

Throughout my life, I had a sense of humor. At Seminole High School, I was a majorette with baton for Powder Puff Football. As a supposed-to-be straight-laced, humorless statistician within the Federal government for 30 years, I orchestrated a bunch of gong shows during the Holidays. I also dressed for Halloween at work— and trick-and-treated for candy. If no candy, a squirt in the face with a squirt gun! I was Count Dracula, Jason with chainsaw, a pirate, a cowboy, and in drag as the "Viagra saleslady". In Federal service, I was sometimes required to take extra classes on sensitivity since my jokes often got me in hot water. At the national convention of the Crown Victoria Association, in front of a crowd of 500, I organized the "FOMOCO SISTERS". Four guys, dressed in drag, sang "Stand By Your Man". I was simply stunning in my black dress with white polka dots, white gloves, wig, makeup, and glittery earrings.

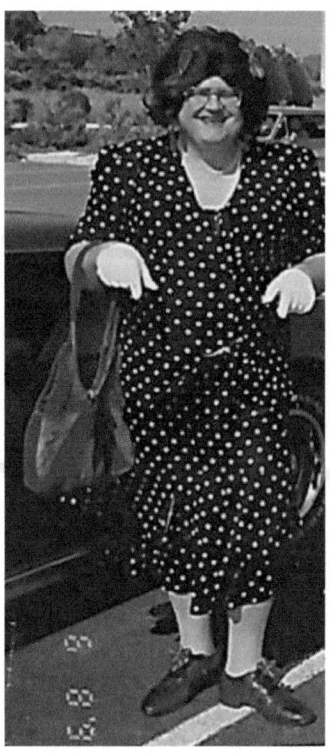

THE AUTHOR IN DRAG

Note that some jokes are two lines long, and some are one full page long. Those each count as one of the 1,000 jokes. Other jokes may have five parts. They each count as five jokes, since you have five chances to smile or laugh. Also, I created a new caption for every joke. OK? Now, enjoy!!!

Yours in good humor,

Paul J. Placek, B.S., M.S., Ph.D.

TABLE OF CONTENTS

Thomas Jay McCahill III (1907–1975) was my favorite automotive journalist when I was younger because of his humorous style of writing. No writer has surpassed him since. He was born into wealth, got a degree in fine arts from Yale University. He raced a series of cars (including a 1952 Cadillac 62, a Carrera Panamericana-spec Lincoln, and an early Thunderbird) in NASCAR's Daytona speed trials. He is credited with coming up with the "0 to 60" acceleration measurement, which is universally accepted in acceleration tests. He also coined the phrase "idiot lights" to refer to Detroit's dash gauges.

MCCAHILL: 23 QUIPS • BALD-FACED LIE • MR. KNOW-IT-ALL • RACING CHAMPIONS: 18 HUMOROUS TRUTHS • TENSE • DRIVER WISDOM • TOO GOOD TO BE TRUE • MECHANIC WISDOM • FIVE RACE CAR DRIVER PROBLEMS, WITH MECHANICS' SOLUTIONS • THE DOWN SIDE • "THE REAL" JIMMY JOHNSON • VERY DARK HUMOR • INDIANAPOLIS ETIQUETTE • PEDRO AND JUAN PABLO, RACE CAR DRIVERS

CHAPTER FIVE. BRAND (DIS)LOYALTY AND ACRONYMS

Did you know that some drivers are passionate about their cars, and equally hate other brands? Consider these jokes.

PSYCHOLOGICAL BIAS • HONEY, IF I DIED... • APOLOGY • PARTY LOYALTY TEST • CAR TIME • SCOTSMAN IS 1/16TH CHEROKEE • IQ TEST • TAKING CANDY • CHEVIES ARE MORE BETTER • LUCAS ANOTHER LUCAS • BRITISH TRIUMPH • HEATED TAILGATES • FREE DOG • OLD VOLKSWAGEN'S GO... • RUSSIAN LADA • USER'S MANUAL • YUGO CHALLENGE • CAR JOKE • PATTY CRASHED 454 MONTE CARLO • JAMES' PROMISE • FORD VS. CHEVY • BEST ACRONYMS FOR POPULAR AMERICAN CARS • AUTHOR'S ACRONYMS FOR 59 OTHER CARS • FORD GUY VS. CHEVY GUYS

CHAPTER SIX. IT'S TOOL TIME!

Every auto aficionado loves tools, whether handy with them or not...

TWENTY-TWO TOOLS • DEALING WITH TRAUMA • BAD TRIP • UNLOVED? • BUILDER A FEW SCREWS SHORT • MECHANIC WHO FELL • LONELY DRILL • STUMPED ENGINEERS • DULL MECHANIC • POPE'S FAVORITE • CAR REPAIR RULES • WIFE'S COMPLAINT • OOPS!

CHAPTER SEVEN. SALUTE TO JEFF FOXWORTHY

With his books, CD's and standup comedy, Jeff Foxworthy has done a stellar job of defining rednecks' personalities, dating habits, lifestyle, quirks, and how they view their autos.

JEFF FOXWORTHY SAYS "TEN HINTS YOU ARE A REDNECK" • STILL TEN MORE WAYS TO ID A REDNECK, SAYS FOXWORTHY • FOXWORTHY HAS YET ANOTHER TEN TIPS ON REDNECKS • WASN'T IT FOXWORTHY WHO SAID YOU NEED NEW WHEELS WHEN...? • WOW, MORE JEFF! • TEN MORE TIPS THAT YOU MIGHT BE A REDNECK BY JEFF FOXWORTHY • AND FINALLY TWO THINGS THAT A REDNECK WILL NEVER SAY...

CHAPTER EIGHT. GOOD OL' BOYS DEFINED

Jeff Foxworthy has described The American "Redneck". I, however, will describe an alternate creature, the American "Good Ol' Boy". Please see three illustrations of the Good Ol' Boy as depicted by the illustrator, Shelby Rehn.

DESCRIPTION OF GOOD OL' BOYS • THE DUKES OF HAZZARD • ANOTHER VERSION OF "GOOD OL' BOYS" • TRAILER-LESS GOOD OL' BOYS • GOOD OL' BOY RULE • GOOD OL' BOY WISDOM • GOOD OL' BOY REPAIRS • GOOD OL' BOYS BEAR LEFT • GOOD OL' BOYS AND BONDS • GOOD OL' BOYS AND READING • FLAT TARR • TEN GOOD OL' BOY RULES FER RIDIN' SHOTGUN* • THINGS GOOD OL'

BOYS DON'T SAY • GOOD OL' BOY FROM KAHOOTS • DADDY AND DARLA • MOLOTOV GOOD OL' BOY • AM/PM • SMART OL' BOY? • FORGETFUL • CAR CLUB DUES • ZUCCHINI • OL' BOY'S CHOICE • WATCH BATTERIES INSTALLED • HAVING A BALL • GOOD OL' BOY AT BAD DRIVER'S SCHOOL • DEVOTION • STRIP DOWN • WARREN JUNOR'S BIKE RIDE • OL' BOY AT DEMO DERBY • GOOD OL' BOYS CRUISE-IN ON JULY 4TH • FLY U.S. AIRLINES Y'ALL • BACK DIRECTLY FROM YONDER FOR MY "MESS A GREENS" • GOOD OL' BOY AT A REDLIGHT • GOOD OL' BOY WORKERS • LAST WORDS OF FRED, A GOOD OL' BOY • BACKATCHA • DEFINITION OF A BOOGER • ALLIGATOR SHOES • OVERKILL • DARE DEVIL • DELANEY'S GOOD OL' BOYS CAR SHOW • DELANEY'S GOOD OL' BOY CAR SHOW (CONT'D) • DELANEY'S LAST UPDATE TO HIS PREVIOUS LAST UPDATE • FROZEN OL' BOYS • OL' BOY THIEF • NTSA'S BLACKBOX • PIG!

CHAPTER NINE. AUTO AFICIONADOS AND HIGHER POWERS 79

The Webster dictionary defines "Higher Powers" as spirits or beings (such as God) which have great power, strength, knowledge, etc. that can affect nature and the lives of people. In this chapter, we take a comical look at fictitious aficionados who attempt to negotiate life, death, wealth, or power with higher entities.

PROPHESY • FAITH • THE TEST • LET US PRAY • MOSES' CHOICE • HELP ON THE WAY • THE MINISTER AND THE SCOTCH • PRIEST GOT HIM ANYWAY • ANYTHING FOR A TROPHY • DON GARLITS GOLFING • TIME WARP • HENRY FORD AT THE PEARLY GATES • TOBY, JIM, AND JOHNNY MEET ST. PETER • EARNHARDT, JOHNSON AND TURNER MEET ST. PETER • JUST REWARD • GOODNESS OVERFLOWS • CAREFUL WHAT YOU WISH FOR • IT'S THE PRAYERS THAT COUNT • LEE IACOCCA AT THE PEARLY GATES • MEDDLING PREACHER • VOCABULARY • A BIG THANK YOU • LIKE CHANGING PEE INTO GAS? • TRUST IN GOD • CAR GUY PRAYER • LOST IN A TORNADO • TOO MANY BLESSINGS • THE GOOD THIEF • TO DUST YE SHALL RETURN • FOR THE SICK • PROMISE BIG • PREACHER SAW THE LIGHT • PETTY, FOYT, AND BUSCH BEAT SATAN • EDSEL FORD AT THE GATES OF HELL • PALMIST • WISH FOR THE GENIE • SAINT PETER WRITES A LETTER • FOUR RIDDLES: CARS IN THE BIBLE

CHAPTER TEN. AUTO AFICIONADOS DEAL WITH EARTHLY AUTHORITIES (POLICE, JUDGES, FIREMEN, ETC.) 98

In a more "down to earth" realm, aficionados must risk daily encounters with police, judges, clerks at the motor vehicle administration, firemen, drunks, thieves, and other close encounters of the second kind while on the highway. In this book, all encounters will make you chuckle.

HARD JUDGE • 50 DOLLARS • JUST ANOTHER DRUNK • GOOD EXCUSE #1 • GOOD EXCUSE #2 • DUMB CAR THIEVES • THE JAILBIRD'S LESSON • DESCRIPTION NEEDED • DREW AT THE MVA • SHELBY SPEEDING DOWN THE HIGHWAY • COMMANDER COMMANDEERED • STOP HIM! • MAKES YOUR HEART RACE • DISTRACTIONS • ROOKIE TRAVIS • DESIGNATED DRIVER FUN • BOTH CHARGED FIFTH ON FOURTH • THE COLLECTION OFFICER • BILLY JOEL'S FAVORITE JOKE • STOLEN CAR • TO AMUSE YOURSELF • WATER TO WINE? • CLOSER • PATRIOTISM • TIPS • BAD SPELLER? • TOO MANY TICKETS • I KNOW DA' GUY • DUELING PHOTOS • SOOOO OBEDIENT • MAKE UP YOUR MIND • TRUE POLICE STORY • TOO DRUNK • SMART ALEC RYAN • REPEAT OFFENDER • ILLEGAL TURN • NO MONEY FOR GAS TO MAKE THE VAN GO • A BRIDGE TOO LOW • MISSED THE TREES? • A FALLING OUT • PULL OVER • NEW SOBRIETY TEST? • MISSING BODY • VIRGINIA COP NABS DEBBIE • ID • SCARF! • A SENSITIVE OFFICER • CARDIAC ARREST? • TREASURED ONE PATTY MISSING • SEVEN THINGS *NOT* TO SAY TO A POLICE OFFICER • SIX POLICE BACKATCHA'S • COPS ARE FUNNY SIX TIMES OVER • FROM FOUR POLICE RECORDINGS OF ARRESTS • WESTERN AUTO CHATTER • ONE-WAY

DEFINED • KEEP THAT CAR • SEVENTEEN ACTUAL STATEMENTS FROM INSURANCE FORMS: DRIVERS DESCRIBED THE ACCIDENT • WOULDN'T GIVE A DOLLAR FOR IT (True Story) • 0-200 GIFT • LOCKER ROOM TALK • PAYBACK • NICE BOYFRIEND? • AUTOBIOGRAPHY • VERY ORIGINAL DATE • MISSED THE POINT • BE HONEST WITH YOUR WIFE

CHAPTER SIXTEEN. CRUISERS AT THE WATERING HOLE

Watering holes are bars, cafes, cantinas, dram shops, gin mills, grogshops, pubs, saloons, taprooms, and/or taverns. The Webster dictionary defines "watering hole" as "...a bar, nightclub, or other social gathering place where alcoholic drinks are sold." Jokesters always begin with "a man walked into a bar", and we immediately grin. Add to that grin our automotive punch lines and you will grin twice!

CHAPTER SEVENTEEN. CRUISIN' AND MAN'S BEST FRIEND

Unquestionably, man's best friend is his dog. As anyone who has one can testify, dogs not only understand us, but they also have uncanny understandings of the ways that vehicles affect our (and their) lives. Find out how! Bow wow! Now!

CHAPTER EIGHTEEN. WIT AND WISDOM

Wisdom includes abiding by accepted mottos, rules, widespread beliefs, brilliant thoughts, answers to the big questions in life, important lessons which people learn the hard way, and/or obedience to a Dad's directives. Wisdom can include adherence to Chinese proverbs or government directives (or else!). Even car club newsletter editors have rules to obey and hence must exhibit wisdom to their readers versed in proper English, southern slang, car talk, redneck slang, and good ol' boy lingo. Ridiculous riddles, rules, rejoinders, rigmarole, riprap, rollickings and rubrics for auto aficionados.

CHAPTER ONE

INTRODUCTION: HUMOR ABOUT OLD CARS AND CAR GUYS WHO ARE OLDER THAN DIRT

We start with surprising myths and gentle humor about the beginnings of the auto in America. A quiz will test whether you are "older than dirt", and we tickle your funny bone about Henry Ford.

"YOU CAN HAVE ANY COLOR AS LONG AS IT'S BLACK"

HA! NOT SO! It is a wisecrack attributed to Henry Ford.

True? *In his book "My Life and Work" by Henry Ford in collaboration with Samuel Crowther, Ford stated that he made the above quip.*

False? *Henry Ford's (1863-1947) first production models were identified by the letters A to T. The Model A's (1903-1904) were in red. The Model F was dark green with yellow running gear. The Model K was royal blue. The Model R was red. Model T's were built from 1909 to 1927 (and 15 million were built)...and the 15 millionth Model T was green with black fenders. (oplaunch.com/blog/2015/04/30/the truth about my color so long as it's black).*

"THE USA IS THE HOME OF THE MOTOR CAR"

HA! NOT SO!

True? In 1908, Henry Ford introduced the assembly line for the Model T to efficiently bring the price down. Soon, half of all cars in America were Model T's.

False? In 1902, only 314 cars were made in America, but in the most productive country (France), 23,000 cars were made. (www.hyerwrite.com/Articles/showarticle.aspx?id=90).

The Model T became known as the "Tin Lizzie" and the "Flivver". Many jokes celebrated the Model T's sturdiness, reliability, and homeliness. These jokes amused Henry Ford such that he stated that every Ford joke sold more cars. So, let's get to some jokes.

DELUXE '41 FORD OR A CHICKEN?

Henry Ford, an eccentric millionaire, in 1941, sent an employee around Detroit to interview the householders. To every man who was really the boss of his house, he was to give a brand new 1941 Ford Deluxe Convertible. To every man who was henpecked, he would give a chicken. Everywhere the employee went, he handed out chickens with never an occasion to give anyone a '41 Ford. Finally, he arrived at the house of a sturdy-looking farmer with a deep voice and muscles like a strongman. In the background was his skinny, quiet wife. The employee said, "Are you the boss in your family, sir?" The worker leaned his head back and bellowed "You bet, little man," he said. "What I say around here goes." And he flexed his muscles to show. "Great," said Ford's employee. "You get a prize. Do you want a red or a blue 1941 Ford?" The he-man asks his wife: "Honey, you want a red or a blue 1941 Ford?" "Definitely, a blue one," she sweetly said." "Whoops," said the Ford employee, "You get a chicken!"

(adapted from www.energyenhanement.org).

MILLIONAIRE BABY

"Q. Why is the Ford like a millionaire baby?

A. Because it has a new rattle every day."

FORD RHYME

"A gallon of gasoline and a quart of oil,

A piece of wire to make a coil,

An old tin can and a piece of board,

And there you are, you have a Ford."

WHERE A MODEL T WILL GO

"A Model T Ford will go anywhere except in society."

(The three "Tin Lizzie" jokes and two vintage postcards are from The Rice's Model T; https://t1920.webs.com/).

Now, for some of MY jokes:

THE GOOD OLD DAYS

At a car show, an old geezer was looking at a Model T and said to the owner: "This car reminds me of the good old days." The owner asked him: "What were the good old days like?" The old geezer replied: "When I wasn't old, and I wasn't good."

CRANK SLIPPED

Walking down the street one day, I spied a man looking up and standing by a tree. I was curious, and looking up, I saw a Model T Ford car in the top of the tree! I asked the man how it got there and he said, "Why, I was cranking it extra hard and it slipped out of my hand."

HISTORY LECTURE

Instructor: "Transportation has progressed increasingly in the modern world. First the horse, then the bicycle, then the Model T Ford, then the Model A Ford, then the V-8, and the muscle cars—and what comes after the muscle cars?" (The instructor hoped students would say "Hybrids", or "Electric cars", but no...). A student shouted out: "Cop cars!"

RUMBLE SEAT

Bay City Bob bought a 1930 Model A Ford with a mother-in-law rumble seat, and he fixed most everything to make it run good except the large rust hole in the floor under the rumble seat. His mother-in-law came to visit and demanded a ride immediately, over Bob's protests. During the ride, the mother-in-law fell through the rust hole and was injured and insulted. Later, whenever a woman would whisper something, then Bob would nod his head yes sympathetically. But whenever a guy would whisper something, he would shake his head no emphatically. Curious, his buddy Paul asked about that. Bay City Bob replied: "The women would say, 'What a horrible accident' and I would quietly agree and say, 'Yes, it was.' The men would ask, 'How much to buy that car?' and I would shake my head and respond, 'Nope, I can make more money renting it out by the week'."

OLDER THAN DIRT QUIZ FOR CAR GUYS

Count all the ones that you actually personally remember from the 1950's, not the ones you were told about. Ratings at the bottom.

Nash (1950-57)

Desoto (1928-1961)

Rambler (1957-59)

Hudson (through 1957)

Kaiser (through 1955)

Henry J (1951-54)Willys (1952-55)

Frazer (1950-51)

Packard (through 1958)

Allstate (sold by Sears Roebuck in 1952-53)

Edwards America (1953-55)

Muntz Jet (1951-54)

Crosley (1949-52)

Studebakers (through 1954)

Cunningham C-3 (1953-55)

If you remember 0-3 = you're still young

If you remember 3-6 = you are getting older

If you remember 7-10 = don't tell your age

If you remember 11-15 = you're older than dirt!

UNFOUNDED FORD RUMOR

It's rumored that old Henry Ford was a stern taskmaster and did not like to hear complaints. In fact, it is thought that his policy was to only allow employees to complain once every five years, and when they did, to only allow them *two words*. An employee got an appointment with Ford after being in his employ for five years. He walked into Ford's office, and Ford told him to say his piece, but just in two words. The employee said: "low pay". Henry Ford said: "That's enough. Out!" The employee departed, but like clockwork, returned to see Henry Ford five years later. Ford said: "Spit it out son, but two words only." The employee said: "No raise", and quickly left. Five years later, at year 15, that same employee went to see Henry Ford, and said: "More money!" "Out," said Ford. Finally, at year 20, that same employee walked in, angry, and said to Henry Ford: "I quit!" Ford responded: "That does not surprise me one bit. You've been complaining around here for 20 years!"

CHAPTER TWO

IN THE INTEREST OF MARITAL HARMONY

There are growing numbers of women as officers of car clubs, at car shows, and at classic car auctions. It's not just a family activity to maintain marital harmony. It's a great way to meet new and interesting friends. Like men, women can develop emotional attachment to a particular car. Male aficionados sometimes buy a second collector car which the wife specifically wants, wheels which express her personality and style. Still, auto obsession seems to be a male-dominated disease.

The reasons? Most (97.9%) of auto mechanics are men, according to the Bureau of Labor Statistics. The American Automobile Association survey found that men drive 2,314 more miles annually than women, and spend 18% more hours behind the wheel. According to Kelly Blue Book, when buying a new car, the average horse power men choose is 360 HP, as compared with 170 HP for women. Cars are not just transportation. They are often an extension of the self or a status symbol. Sometimes cars are named, and become "friends" with their own personalities. Think of the movie "Christine", in which the 1958 Plymouth Fury bonded to its owner's personality. Think of "Herbie", a mischievous VW Bug which had a mind of its own. Think of the Knight Rider series, in which a Pontiac Trans Am named "KITT", was self-aware, high-tech, and indestructible. Think of "Cars", the Disney/ Pixar computer-animated film with over 25 talking cars, including a 1951 Hudson and a 1951 International Harvester tow truck. Witness the vanity tags (or person- alized plates) which describe the car or the owner. "The tie that binds" is a factor or shared belief that links people together. I think that it includes a person who bonds with a cherished car. Better yet, a collector car can bond a couple together in a fun mutual interest. Even better, couples can tease and taunt each other about rules for collecting old cars and laugh about whether the Ten Commandments for Car Collectors apply at their house. Since it's hard to say and harder to spell "aficionados", we'll just call them "car guys".

JUST FOR THE LADIES

Ladies...are you married to "Car Guy"? If yes, here are some survival tips.

1. When requesting to accompany Car Guy for a country drive, be very specific as to your destination, since he thinks that short trips and outings should include scanning the local junkyards for unique and usable parts.

2. When requesting Car Guy to go to Walmart for lotions or oils, ask that he NOT spend more than one hour in the automotive section.

3. To gain eye contact from Car Guy, just say the words "look at that neat old car," which will provoke him to at least look your way for a split second. This, of course, does not guarantee interaction from Car Guy.

4. To persuade Car Guy into paying you some amorous attention, it is important to wear something in Ford Blue or Viper Red.

5. Once amorous attention has been gained, incorporate the automotive language into your requests: "I need a tune up!"; "My motor's heating up."

6. For better yard care services from Car Guy, install a Ford steering wheel on his riding mower. Also flames.

7. For pleasant dinners at home, purchase special plates and glasses with car models on them.

8. Always show excitement and gratitude for his gifts of earrings and necklaces with cars on them. After all he did think of you!

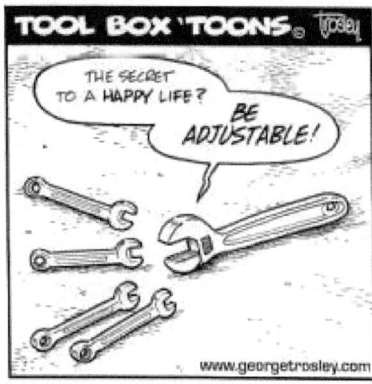

ADVICE FROM THE AUTHOR

Many readers of this book are car collectors. Therefore, as someone who has owned over 30 old cars and has been happily married 42 years, I have guidance for the novice on how to keep your wife happy.

TEN COMMANDMENTS FOR THE CAR COLLECTOR*

"1. Thou shalt not store thy cars out-of-doors, except for thy wife's modern iron.

2. Thou shalt not covet thy neighbor's car, nor his car trailer, nor his garage, nor his battery charger.

3. Thou shalt not love thy cars more than thy wife and children: As much, but not more.

4. Thou shalt not read thy car magazines on company time, lest thy employer make it impossible to continue thy car payments.

5. Thou shalt not despise thy neighbor's Edsel, nor his DeSoto, nor even his 1947 Plymouth.

6. Thou shalt not allow thy daughters nor thy sons to get married during the Holy Days of Carlisle.

7. Thou shalt not deceive thy wife into thinking that thou art taking her for a romantic Sunday drive when, indeed, thou art going out to look at another car.

8. Thou shalt not tell thy spouse the entire cost of thy latest restoration, at least not all at the same time.

9. Thou shalt not promise thy wife a new addition to the house and then use it to store cars; thou shalt not store cars in the attic.

10. Thou shalt not buy thy wife a floor jack for Christmas."

*Donald R. Peterson; http://www.richiezie.com/ten-commandments-car-collectors-live-by;

http://www.wheelman.com/TenCommandments.html; https://www.camaros.net/forums/11-bench-racing/72120-ten-commandments-car-collector.html; https://www.corvetteforum.com/forums/c1-and-c2-corvettes/1586955-ten-commandments-for-the-car-collector.html; http://www.cyber-wiz-ard.ca/2011/05/04/ten-commandments-for-car-collectors/

We continue with advice for Rednecks, Good Ol' Boys, Car Guys, and collectors of old cars such that marital bliss may be preserved.

TEN RULES FOR COLLECTING OLD CARS

RULE 1: Collect only one make and model of old car. When all your old cars are the same shape, it's harder for anyone to figure out just how many old cars you have.

RULE 2: Never line up all your old cars together. Nothing distresses a spouse more than seeing eight old cars lined up, looking like wasted money. Scatter the old cars around here and there.

RULE 3: Give your old cars the same names. You'd be surprised how much less trouble you will have if you name them all "Mildred".

RULE 4: When you start to collect old cars, buy a car you don't want. Then sell it as quickly as you can. Don't worry about making any money on the transaction. The main thing is to buy a car and get rid of it. Then you can say "I'm thinking of selling another one any day now, so we can put your new car in the garage."

RULE 5: Pay for your old cars with cash or postal money orders, which hides the evidence. Then eat the stubs, carbon copies or receipts immediately.

RULE 6: Now and then buy a wreck for "parts" even if you don't need the parts. That makes you sound like an investment wizard.

RULE 7: Plan to drag home a car without a transmission or rear wheels. Then say: "That's no car, that's only for parts."

RULE 8: Ask friend Skip to leave a message on your answering machine so your wife can retrieve it. The friend should say: "Bob told me to keep an eye on the old car going at the Mecum auction, but it sold for $5,000 and I know there's no way a responsible fellow like Bob would pay that much. So I refrained from bidding on it for him." This makes you look financially responsible. Then, in the future, when you buy an old car, say: "Sugar plum, this old car only cost me $10,000 which means we are $5,000 ahead of where we would have been if I let Skip get me the one before.

RULE 9: If your mate asks "Who do you love more, me or your old cars?", don't ask for time to think it over! Shout "YOU!" Also, do not leave the phone number of the County Zoning Department around. She may turn you in.

RULE 10: Hide your car behind other car parts, old refrigerators, and construction debris. Clean people will not want to go there and snoop around. And hide these rules from your spouse!

Some guys have very thick heads and drool uncontrollably around vintage cars. Therefore, we provide clear guidelines on what NOT to give your wife for her birthday. Copy them and hang this list up on the side of your tool chest.

TOP TEN GIFTS YOUR WIFE DOESN'T WANT FOR HER BIRTHDAY

10. A car wash kit

9. A 5 HP, 80 gallon air compressor

8. Two all-day passes to Cars at Carlisle

7. A case of high mileage engine oil

6. Five-year subscription to *Hot Rodder* magazine

5. A set of five wide whitewall tires

4. A $50 gift coupon for Dennis Carpenter merchandise

3. A vanity tag with her name on it

2. New satellite dish subscription with My Classic Car and Outdoor Life channels

(And the one which will have you sleeping out in the garage)

1. Three-year membership to Weight Watchers Clinic

CHAPTER THREE

HIGHWAY HUMOR WITH BURMA SHAVE, BILLBOARDS, AND BUMPER STICKERS

In this chapter, we look at humor on the American road. We start with Burma Shave signs, a fixture on most American highways in the 1930's, 1940's and 1950's. Large billboards also became the rage, until they were controlled. Then, outrageous signs and bumper stickers became popular and free speech is still alive and well. Finally, we briefly conclude with humor on vanity tags. We will start with Burma Shave.

ON THE HIGHWAY WITH BURMA SHAVE

Burma Shave is part of our history from the 1930s, '40s, and '50s. Everyone drove on two-lane roads. Interstate highways did not exist until 1956. Burma Shave signs would be posted in most states in the countryside. The essential oils in Burma Shave actually did come from Burma. The formula was five signs, 100 feet apart, each with one line of a four line couplet...and the final fifth sign promoting Burma Shave. The sign posts were nine feet long with three feet buried! They had to be lengthened to get the seven feet off the ground because horses used the signs to scratch their backs, which knocked the signs down. The red signs were ten feet high by three feet long, with four inch white letters.

There were 600 different Burma Shave rhymes with a total of 7,000 sets of signs across the USA. Most were written by Allan and Clinton Odell. Later, contests were done, with up to 50,000 entries for the $100 prize.

Some of the best-selling Burma-Shave books include: 1) Verse by the Side of the Road, by Frank Rowsome. 2) Sunday Drives: Nostalgic Reminiscing with The Best of Burma-Shave, by Michael Larson and Jill Larson Sundberg. 3) Burma-Shave: The Rhymes, The Signs, The Times, by Bill Vossler.

Rhymes which follow are from the above sources.

"Don't Lose Your Head

To Gain a Minute

You Need Your Head

Your Brains Are In It

Burma Shave

Drove Too Long

Driver Snoozing

What Happened Next

Is Not Amusing

Burma Shave

Brother Speeder

Let's Rehearse

All Together

Good Morning Nurse

Burma Shave

Cautious Rider

To Her Reckless Dear

Let's Have Less Bull

And More Steer

Burma Shave

Speed Was High

Weather Was Not

Tires Are Thin

X Marks The Spot

Burma Shave

The Midnight Ride

Of Paul For Beer

Led To A Warmer

Hemisphere

Burma Shave

Around the Curve

Lickety-Split

It's A Beautiful Car

Wasn't It?

Burma Shave

No Matter The Price

No Matter How New

The Best Safety Device

In The Car Is You

Burma Shave

A Guy Who Drives

A Car Wide Open

Is Not Thinkin'

He's Just Hopin'

Burma Shave

At Intersections

Look Each Way

A Harp Sounds Nice

But Its Hard To Play

Burma Shave

Both Hands On The Wheel

Eyes On The Road

That's The Skillful

Driver's Code

Burma Shave

The One Who Drives When

He's Been Drinking

Depends On You

To Do His Thinking

Burma Shave

Car In Ditch

Driver In Tree

The Moon Was Full

And So Was He

Burma Shave

Passing School Zone

Take It Slow

Let Our Little

Shavers Grow

Burma Shave"

...and about 600 more!

BILLBOARDS

It has become an American tradition for First Ladies to take up a good cause and promote it during their husbands' Presidential administration. In the case of Lyndon Baines Johnson who became President after JFK's 1963 assassination, wife Lady Bird's pet project was highway beautification. She believed that beautiful highways would make this country a better place to live. "Lady Bird's Bill" was the Highway Beautification Act of 1965, and it required control and removal of certain types of billboards and signs along interstate and federal highways. Gadzooks! Even junkyards along interstates or main highways had to be removed or screened. Nonetheless, some billboards have survived. Check out a few.

www.oddee.com

www.twentytwowords.com

www.conwaydailysun.com

DUE TO SPACE LIMITATIONS, YOU WILL JUST HAVE TO USE THE TEXT BELOW TO IMAGINE THE COLOR AND INGENUITY OF THE FOLLOWING BILLBOARDS…

EIGHT FUNNY BILLBOARDS

1. SEX! NOW THAT WE HAVE YOUR ATTENTION, EAT AT _____

2. ALCOHOL. IT'S CHEAPER THAN THERAPY. _____ DISCOUNT LIQUOR STORE

3. YOUR WIFE IS HOT. GET YOUR AUTO AC CHECKED OUT AT _____'S GARAGE

4. WE'D LOVE TO BE SITTING ON YOUR FACE. _____ SUNGLASSES

5. DON'T READ THIS BILLBOARD WHILE DRIVING. DISTRACTION KILLS!

6. ILLITERATE? WRITE FOR FREE HELP (P.O. Box ____)

7. FROM CRASH TO CASH. Call Attorney (name and phone)

8. DISLIKE COPS? WHEN YOU NEED HELP, CALL A HIPPIE

ROAD SIGNS

Fortunately, we also have road signs to amuse us. Check out a few which follow.

www.americanroadmagazine.com

Vifreepress.com

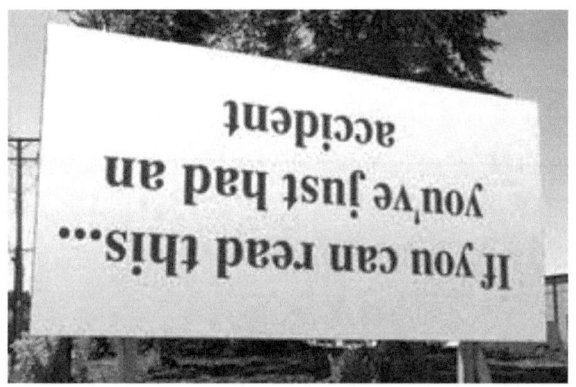

www.bbcamerica.com

www.arrivealive.mobi

www.luxledsigns.com

FREE SEX WITH TEN GALLONS OR MORE

At Homer's Friendly Gas Station in Kentucky, Homer was trying to increase sales. Homer had a big sign painted which said: "FREE SEX WITH 10 GALLONS OR MORE."

Good ol' boy Booney drove in, filled the tank of his pick 'em up, and asked Homer about getting the free sex. Homer told him to pick a number from 1 to 5, and if that was the number he was thinking of today, he could have the free sex. Booney thought hard and blurted out: "Number 3". "Sorry," said Homer, the number today was 2. Try another day. The next day good ol' boy Booney drove up to the station in an old Jeep, with his pretty girlfriend with him. After his Jeep was filled with gas, Homer gave him a chance to pick a number from 1 to 5, and if he picked the number that Homer was thinking of, he could get free sex. "Number 4", said Booney. "Sorry, the number was 5", said Homer. "No free sex today."

As they were driving away, Booney said to his girlfriend: "I hate to accuse Homer, but I think his game is rigged and no one ever wins. He just runs that game to increase gas sales." Booney's girlfriend protested innocently with wide eyes: "That game ain't rigged, Booney, I played it and won twice in a row."

ENTER HERE

A used car dealer was dismayed when another car dealership opened up next door. The new dealership installed a huge sign that said "BEST DEALS!" To make things even worse, another used car dealer opened on his other side with a huge sign reading "LOWEST PRICES!" He nearly despaired until he thought up the idea for his new sign, a huge one, which read, "ENTER HERE!"

SEVENTEEN SIGNS, SIGNS, EVERYWHERE A SIGN...

JOHN'S SEPTIC PUMPING – We pump yesterday's meals on wheels.

PETER'S PORTO-POTTIES – We've #1 in the #2 business.

DEYOUNG TOWING – We don't charge an arm and a leg. We want toes!

SKIP'S WRECKER SERVICE – We meet by accident.

VINCE'S ELECTRIC SERVICE – Let us remove your shorts.

PAUL'S TIRE SHOP – Invite us to your next blowout.

OTTO'S VULC-RITE TIRE CO. – Time to re-tire.

DUTY'S AUTO REPAIRS – We fix what your husband fixed.

PICK-A-PART SALVAGE YARD – Drive recklessly. It helps business!

HONEST BOB'S USED CARS – The best way to take long healthy walks is to miss a car payment!

DUTY'S MUFFLER SHOP – No appointment needed, we hear you coming.

LERNER'S RADIATOR SERVICE – Best place to take a leak.

DOTTIE'S CAR WASH – We give the best hand job in town.

BIG DADDY'S TEXACO – Let us give you the business.

ROBB'S DIFFERENTIAL SERVICE – Let us lube your rear end.

BIG MIKE'S WIRING – We won't shock you with our work.

BILLY'S JUNKYARD – All cars run on used parts. Why not use ours?

BUMPER STICKERS

Fortunately, if there aren't enough road signs to keep us laughing, there are also bumper stickers.

FOUR BUMPER STICKERS

1. Hang up and drive!

2. Change the world – use your turn signals.

3. ALL CAPITAL LETTERS MEANS I'M SERIOUS

4. Not too close. I'm not that kind of car.

THREE TEEN DRIVER BUMPER STICKERS

1. If You Drink, DRIVE...Don't Park, Because Accidents Cause People.

2. How Many Roads Must A Man Travel Down Before He Admits He is Lost?

3. So Many Pedestrians—So Little Time.

SIX BUMPER STICKERS SEEN ON JEEPS

1. You can drive faster but this macho machine can go anywhere.

2. My mind was never changed by a bumper sticker.

3. Paved road are an example of wasteful government spending.

4. When the road ends, the fun begins.

5. Don't follow me. You won't make it.

6. My Jeep is using what your hybrid is using.

ELEVEN BODACIOUS BUMPER STICKERS

1. Yes, this is my truck.

No, I won't help you move.

2. Another whiner for world peace.

3. Watch out for the idiot behind me.

4. My mind was changed by a bumper sticker—not!

5. A planet is a terrible thing to waste.

6. Warning – Driver has road rage.

7. Flatheads Forever.

8. Loud pipes save lives.

9. If it won't go – chrome it!

10. If it isn't broken – take it apart and fix it!

11. State bird of Pennsylvania – the traffic cone!

SCARY MOM BUMPER STICKERS

"**1. My child is average with very little ambition.**

2. I pick my nose at stoplights – watch!

3. I'm a terrible driver steer clear.

4. If I smile at you at a stoplight – I'm farting.

5. Jesus might not love you. He saw what you did last night.

6. If you get any closer you will need to buy me a drink.

7. I only let people I like touch my tailpipe."

(shop.scarymommy.com)

ELEVEN ZAZZLES

"**1. Diapers and politicians should both be changed often (for the same reason).**

2. There's no problem that the government can't make worse.

3. Sorry for driving so close in front of you.

4. My opinions are so insightful that you should read them while you follow me.

5. It was me. I let the dogs out.

6. A tailgater bought me this car. What to buy my next one?

7. The closer you get, the slower I go.

8. Friction is a drag.

9. Authorized vehicle.

10. Go around, this is obviously not a Corvette.

11. If this truck is rockin' don't come knockin."

(Source: www.zazzle.com)

VANITY TAGS

Personalized license plates are yet another source of amusement as we wander American roads. Some of the more amusing tags which I have seen while out and about are these:

WAS HIS (a divorce prize?)

VLAD THE (on an Impala)

LEMON (getting back at the manufacturer)

WELFARE (on a Cadillac)

A64BIRD (on author's 1964 Thunderbird)

9TEEN55 (on author's 1955 Ford)

LDIABLO (on author's black 1949 Hudson with custom demonic hood ornament. LDIABLO means 'the devil' in Spanish).

There are 276 million registered vehicles in America. Each state offers the option of vanity tags (personalized plates). States vary with what percent of all plates are vanity tags, with a low of 0.5% in Texas to a high of 16% in Virginia (www.nbcnews. com). If about 5% of all tags are vanity tags that would mean 13 million in the USA. Too many to explore in this book! Besides, we only like the clever ones. American creativity has no end! A 1991 book entitled GR8 PL8S: The Best of America's Vanity Plates by Sam G. Riley presented his collection of the most outrageous, cunning, and silly messages on US plates. It included comments on the car (GASHOG, AWESOME), description of their professions (IFLOSS), their interests (HOT4YOU), and their love of animals (CATLUVR).

CONSIDERATE HUSBAND

"Thank you, darling, for being so understanding about me buying my fourth collector car. I actually bought it for you, even though it's a stick shift and you don't like the color," said the husband. "Just for being so nice about it, you can put anything you like on the new vanity tag. Here is the check and the stamped envelope for the Motor Vehicle Administration, ready for you to mail. Just surprise me." Three weeks later, the vanity tag came in the mail. It said: "FOR SALE."

CHAPTER FOUR

TESTING AND RACING CARS

Thomas Jay McCahill III (1907–1975) was my favorite automotive journalist when I was younger because of his humorous style of writing. No writer has surpassed him since. He was born into wealth, got a degree in fine arts from Yale University. He raced a series of cars (including a 1952 Cadillac 62, a Carrera Panamericana-spec Lincoln, and an early Thunderbird) in NASCAR's Daytona speed trials. He is credited with coming up with the "0 to 60" acceleration measurement, which is universally accepted in acceleration tests. He also coined the phrase "idiot lights" to refer to Detroit's dash gauges.

After WW II he wrote 600 articles on a variety of subjects for magazines such as Popular Science, Reader's Digest and Mechanix Illustrated. He was correct in expecting that a post-WWII population was ready for articles on new cars. In 1946, he convinced the editors of Mechanix Illustrated to publish his evaluations. His opinions were fearless, and this endeared him to some in the automotive world. It created enemies as well. From 1946 to 1975, he tested over 600 cars.

In McCahill's test drive of the new 1948 Oldsmobile 98, he stated: "...stomping its gas pedal was like stepping on a wet sponge." This unkind review was the push for Olds engineers to install the new OHV V-8 into the same body. It therefore became the first muscle car after WW II. He published that the 1953 Kaiser car was as comfortable as "a wheelchair upholstered in cream puffs." He wrote that the 1954 De Soto felt "as solid as the Rock of Gibraltar and just as fast."

McCahill referred to himself as "Uncle Tom" and believed he was the greatest automotive journalist, other than his favorite, "Terwilliger Muffinpuss". On the subject of illegal speed as a cause of highway deaths, he said "Phooey!...the four primary causes of our annual roadway slaughter: obsolete highways, stone age police practices, bad drivers and unsafe automobiles." Read some of his other metaphors now.

MCCAHILL: 23 QUIPS

On the AC (Shelby) Cobra:

"...hairier than a Borneo gorilla in a raccoon suit."

On the 1958 Edsel:

"I wouldn't own one except with the export kit. Without stiffer suspension, a car with so much performance could prove similar to opening a Christmas basket full of King Cobras in a small room with the lights out."

On the 1948 Oldsmobile Futuramatic:

Hitting the accelerator was like "...stepping on a wet sponge."

On the 1957 Nash:

"Like steering a three-acre lot..."

On the Checker Cab:

"When you get in the back seat, you are forced to wonder what the boys who built Cadillacs and Lincolns had in mind and where they lost the interior dimensions. There's enough room in the back to carry an embalmed basketball center with his legs straight out."

On the 1949 Dodge with Gyro-Matic Transmission:

"It's a dog."

On the (British) Jowett Javalin's Ashtray:

"...looks like it was invented by Lord Wiffinpoof after he was shot in the rump during the Boer War. Like the cup your favorite dentist tells you to spit your teeth into, hinges out but spends most of Its time just rattling."

On the 1957 FC-150 Jeep:

"...here is a pickup rig capable of carrying a dozen kegs of beer across the icy wastes to starved Laplander reindeer or for smuggling a whole still right out from under the eye of the revenooers."

On the '57 Pontiac:

Ride quality was "as smooth as a prom queen's thighs."

On the '57 Buick:

Handled "like a fat matron trying to get out of a slippery bathtub."

On the 1960 Valiant:

"When equipped with the power pack, they are the hottest cars in the world for under $2500.00.........Gets my vote as the best buy of the three new compacts, and the one I'd most like to own."

On the 1962 Plymouth:

" It was raining like tears in a onion cannery when I did my test.......I don't know of a car in its class that can top Plymouth. It offers the best roadability in its class, and this, tied up with good brakes makes it just about the safest. ....the slightly teutonic looks of the Valiant, enlarged tail lights (on the 62 Plymouth) stand out like a hip flask in a bikini."

On early 30's Classic Imperials:

"These long-hooded brutes had more sex appeal than a boatload of starlets anchored off Alcatraz."

On the 1960 Dodge Dart Phoenix:

"When equipped with the optional D-500 engine, displacing 383 cubic inches with two-four barrel carburetors, it should be able to chew around a race course with enough stuff to turn the humidity into steam.......... (and) make a helluva ridge-runner for the moonshine boys."

On the 1959 Dodge:

"The front end is as new as next February's cold."

On the 1959 Plymouth:

"Plymouth for 1959 is the best car of the low-priced three in our bald-headed opinion, and we've tested all of them."

On the 1959 Imperial:

"This doll was as loaded as an opium peddler during a tong war...Swivel seats make it as easy to get into as a floating crap game with fresh money...On the 31-degree-banked turns, the big Imp hung in there like oil going through a hose... The finest car built in America, and I've been testing cars for a long time."

On Chrysler's famed torsion bar front suspension:

"Chrysler's torsion bar suspension is SO far superior to anything else being made in this country that the contest isn't even close."

On Chrysler's re-designed torqueflite transmission for 1962:

"...features an oil filter to comb out the rocks and dog hair."

On the 1966 Dodge Coronet Hemi:

"With no exception, the blockbuster Hemi 426 is the hairiest full-size stock production car ever tested for these pages...This family-sized rig has all the belt of a two-mile swim in a whiskey vat...When you put your foot through the firewall make sure your teeth are well anchored...It is as furry as a mink farm and as snarly as a Bengal tiger in a butcher shop."

On the 1956 Chrysler Windsor:

"The most car for the dough - for looks, performance, comfort and price."

On the 1957 Imperial:

"The most spectacular looking new car to date..... will get down the pike like a vaselined arrow, and with no more effort than skipping off a cliff."

On the 1962 Chrysler 300:

"I had the car for over a month, and had as many adventures with it as a Siberian trapper would have in Miami Beach. ......The new 300 is the old Windsor, sexed-up and poured into a sport suit.....When you slide behind the wheel you get the feeling that this is a big compact, and not an oversized barge as awkward to handle as wearing moose antlers in a telephone booth..... A functional car that gives top performance with lots of room for beaucoup stuff, which might include wine, weazels or women...... In summing up, the (1962) Chrysler 300 is the best value in the medium-priced field that I have driven in several years."

BALD-FACED LIE

Car shows were always entertaining when Tom McCahill attended. He was bald as a billiard ball. He was once asked how he had become so bald. Tom said he was trying to drive in tight circles, faster and faster, until he drove up his own tailpipe and disappeared! When he did, the sharp edge of the tailpipe cut all his hair off. (NOTE: This tall tale was once told by automotive writer Tom McCahill).

(Mechaniix Illustrated, various years, including March 1957 article, "McCahill Tests the FC-150 Jeep", pp. 90-93 and 170-172; Blog.Modern Mechanix.com/tag/mccahill; www.motortrend.com/news/c12-0603-icons-uncle-tom-mccahill; www.thetruthaboutcars.com/2009/Sutherland; Car Owner Handbook by Tom McCahill, Fawcett Book #310, Greenwich, CT, 1956; What You Should Know About Cars by Tom

McCahill, Fawcett Book #538, Greenwich, CT, 1963; www.hemmings.com/blog/article/tom-mccahill/); https://www.hemmings.com/stories/article/tom-mccahill.

In the April 2001 issue of FOMOCO TIMES, Paul Placek assumed the pseudonym of "Mr. Know-It-All". Placek used clip art from one of Tom McCahill's books to illustrate Placek's personal humor. The following page reproduced courtesy of the President of the Crown Victoria Association, Mr. Toby Gorny.

MR. KNOW-IT-ALL

Mr. Know-It-All

The CVA Advice Column Specially Written for the April, 2001 Issue of Fomoco Times
Mr. Know-It-All is a special friend of the Editor

Dear Mr. Know-It-All:
How can I remove the smell of brake fluid from my wife's frying pan? I used it to clean parts.
Toby G., Bryan, OH

Dear Toby:
First use a good brand of carburetor cleaner, then scrub with lacquer thinner. Finally, wipe down with WD-40 so her pancakes won't stick.
Mr. K
* * * * * * * *

Dear Mr. Know-It-All:
I just rebuilt my Y-Block engine in my '56 Ford and had this big round thing left over with a rod hanging from it. Do you think that's the reason my car won't start?
Mike S, Penndel, PA

Dear Mike:
I forget to put things back in engines all the time, and they won't start either. So that has nothing to do with it. Just whack the carburetor with a big wooden hammer, then coast the car down the hill and pop the clutch. If that fails, call a CVA Tech Advisor!
Mr. K
* * * * * * * * *

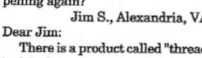

Dear Mr. Know-It-All:
I had a lug nut fall off a wheel. How can I prevent that from happening again?
Jim S., Alexandria, VA

Dear Jim:
There is a product called "thread lock" that you can put on the threads, and it keeps the nut and bolt from ever coming loose. Be careful when you try to loosen it. If you put a long-handled pipe wrench on it, the car will spin around and flip over on you. That would take the big smile right off your face!
Mr. K
* * * * * * * * *

Dear Mr. Know-It-All:
I baked some powder-coated parts in my wife's oven last week and they turned out great. However, the roast she just cooked tasted like chemicals! What do you suggest?
Mick M., Lowell, IN.

Dear Mick:
Tell her the next time that she shops, she should select a better cut of meat. Also buy her a cookbook and gently suggest that she upgrade her cooking skills.
Mr. K

Dear Mr. Know-It-All:
My '56 Meteor is rusty, smelly, and held together with duct tape. How can I win a trophy with it in Des Moines?
Anne B., Ontario

Dear Anne:
I suggest that, on the way, you have a run-in with the Hells Angels, and go for a Hard Luck Trophy.
Mr. K
* * * * * * * * *

Dear Mr. Know-It-All:
I help my father-in-law now and then so he will let me drive his cars. I tried blowing up some tires recently, but they just won't hold air. Any suggestions?
Ken W., Rockaway, NJ

Dear Ken:
Two suggestions for you. If it's a tubeless tire, put it on the rim first. Also, don't try to reuse those tires you used for police target practice!
Mr. K
* * * * * * * * *

Dear Mr. Know-It-All:
Who invented the Ford steering gear and what ever became of him?
Bob H., South Lyon, MI

Dear Bob:
His name is Pittman. he started driving in tight circles, faster and faster, and finally drove right up his own tailpipe and disappeared!
Mr. K
* * * * * * * * *

Dear Mr. Know-It-All:
Whenever I drive past a bunch of telephone poles, I go into a hypnotic trance. I almost wrecked the car last week! My wife says to ignore it. What do you think? Is this vision problem serious?
Paul P., Stevensville, MD

Dear Paul:
Your wife says to ignore this trance thing? I think that she is greedy and trying to collect on your life insurance. For a small fee, I can refer you to my friend Po' Boy, for some 'shine which will totally blur the telephone poles. Or, if your wife is interested, I can refer her to my other brother Vinny, an enforcer in New Jersey. Either way, your vision problem will go away.
Mr. K

PAGE 15

A joke book for auto aficionados would not be complete without these 18 selected humorous quotations about racing or from well-known racers.

RACING CHAMPIONS:
18 HUMOROUS TRUTHS

"Auto racing began five minutes after the second car was built."

— *Henry Ford*

"He ran out of talent about halfway through the corner."

— *Buddy Baker*

"Faster, faster, faster, until the thrill of speed overcomes the fear of death."

— *Hunter Thompson*

"Why worry about death, it'll come sooner or later."

— *Jim Dunn*

"It is amazing how many drivers, even at the Formula One Level, think that the brakes are for slowing the car down."

— *Mario Andretti*

"You can tell that you're in trouble when you feel the air on the back of your neck instead of in your face."

— *Buddy Baker*

"Moonshiners put more time, energy, thought, and love into their cars than any racer ever will. Lose on the track, and you go home. Lose with a load of whiskey, and you go to jail."

— *Junior Johnson, NASCAR legend, and one time whiskey runner*

"You can't fix stupid."

— *Larry Morgan, NHRA Pro Stock driver (Note: Did Ron White of the Blue Collar Comedy Tour borrow this from Larry Morgan?)*

"After the third flip, I lost control..."

— *Don Roberts after crashing in the Jade Grenade at New England Dragway in 1975*

"No, I don't drive her to win, I just drive her as fast as she will go."

— *Juan Fangio*

"Auto racing, bull fighting, and mountain climbing are the only real sports... all the others are games."

— *Ernest Hemingway*

"If you're in control, you're not going fast enough."

— *Parnelli Jones*

"No, no, he didn't slam you, he didn't bump you, he didn't nudge you... he rubbed you. And rubbin, son, is racin'."

— *Harry Hogge, Days of Thunder*

"Speed has never killed anyone, suddenly becoming stationary... that's what gets you."

— *Jeremy Clarkson*

"Aerodynamics are for people who can't build engines."

— *Enzo Ferrari*

"You win some, you lose some, you wreck some."

— *Dale Ernhardt Sr.*

"We broke something, I think it was traction..."

— *Carl Edwards after getting spun out by Dale Jr. at Michigan*

"When I raced a car last it was at a time when sex was safe and racing was dangerous. Now, it's the other way 'round."

— *Hans Stuck*

(www.swartzgarage.com; www.conceptcarz.com; www.clubwix.net; www.zeuslocator.com; www. jayski.com; www.stewarthaasracing.com; www.regroups.com)

TENSE

Did you hear that the Indy 500, past, present, and future drivers walked into the driver's lounge? It was tense.

DRIVER WISDOM

The shortest distance between two points depends on how far apart they are.

TOO GOOD TO BE TRUE

When everything's going your way, you're in the wrong lane.

MECHANIC WISDOM

You haven't had enough coffee until you can adjust the valves on a Y-Block with the valve covers off and the engine running.

FIVE RACE CAR DRIVER PROBLEMS, WITH MECHANICS' SOLUTIONS

After each race, the drivers make "Problem" notes to the mechanics. "Solution" is what the mechanics' solution was. Here are some typical entries after a big race.

Problem: Left front tire almost needs replacement

Solution: Almost replaced left front tire

Problem: Test drive OK except posi-traction grip is poor

Solution: Posi-traction not installed on this car

Problem: Something loose in cockpit

Solution: Something tightened in cockpit

Problem: Dead bugs on windshield

Solution: Live bugs on back-order

Problem: Car goes airborne at 200 MPH

Solution: Cannot reproduce problem in shop

THE DOWN SIDE

At a demolition derby, the track announcer shouts to the crashing cars: "Car Number 99, you are disqualified." He shouts it twice, when his assistant says: "Boss, there is no 99 car. Embarrassed, the announcer grabs his microphone again: "Car 66, are you OK?"

"THE REAL" JIMMY JOHNSON

Author Paul Placek (left) with "The Real" Jimmy Johnson at the East Coast Indoor Nationals, Timonium, Maryland, on December 7, 2019. Jimmy says two things: "Any day is good for stock car racing", and "Please visit Racers Reunion.com and Memory Lane Museum, Mooresville, North Carolina". Jimmy gave Paul permission to reprint his caricature, which follows.

VERY DARK HUMOR

Q: What do Dale Earnhardt and Pink Floyd have in common?

A: Their last big hit was "The Wall".

INDIANAPOLIS ETIQUETTE

Q: Why don't race car drivers eat before a big race?

A: To avoid indy-gestation.

PEDRO AND JUAN PABLO, RACE CAR DRIVERS

In 2005, Pedro Rodriguez and Juan Pablo Garcia, world famous race car drivers, decided to start a new business together. It was to be a bungee-jumping sport in Mexico. With their money, they would buy more powerful engines for their cars. They agreed that this would be a good money maker, and they pooled their money to buy a huge 100' mobile tower, elastic bungee cord, safety harness, insurance, and a big sign in Spanish. They went to Autodome Miquel E. Abed racetrack in Puebla State to demonstrate it. Everyone in the village gathered and they were in a curious and festive mood. The crowd had never before seen such a thing. Pedro and Juan Pablo decided to give the crowd a real show. In their enthusiasm, they forgot to hang their new sign, "EL SALTO DE CAIDA LIBRE" ("BUNGEE JUMPING"). Pedro wore a very colorful outfit and put on his safety harness and snapped it tight to the bungee cord. He also decided to throw candy to the crowd when he fell close to them. He swan-dived off the 100' tower and as he got near to the ground, threw candy and was snapped back away from the ground safely, back up towards Juan Pablo. Pedro again plummeted to near the ground again but sprung back up to Juan Pablo with cuts and scratches and bruises. Juan Pablo was unable to catch him and Pedro plummeted once again and sprung back up with even more damage to his body—bloody nose and much bruising. At the top, Juan Pablo caught him and asked: "What happened? Was the cord too long?" Pedro replied: "No, the cord was perfect, but the crowd thought I was a piñata!"

CHAPTER FIVE.

BRAND (DIS)LOYALTY AND ACRONYMS

Did you know that some drivers are passionate about their cars, and equally hate other brands? Consider these jokes.

PSYCHOLOGICAL BIAS

A psychologist was visiting the Empire State Building and took an elevator to the top. There on the ledge was a fellow about to jump. "Stop!", shouted the doctor. The fellow hesitated and pulled back. "I'm a skilled psychologist, and I can help you. Just a few questions, please…" "OK, shoot," said the fellow. "OK," said the psychologist, "Do you like classic cars?" "Sure, I love them," the fellow said. "Me too," said the psychologist. "Ford or Chevy?" "Ford, said the fellow. "Classic mid-50's or late 60's muscle cars?", asked the psychologist. "Mid-1950's, said the fellow, as the psychologist smiled approvingly. "Don't think that the 1956 Crown Victoria is the most stylish car ever designed?" "Absolutely!" cried the fellow in total approval. Then the fellow seemed to reconsider… "Except, I think that the 1956 Chevy Nomad wagon has better styling." The psychologist immediately pushed the fellow off the ledge, screaming: "Die, you traitor."

HONEY, IF I DIED…

Husband: Honey! I've read that men die seven years before women. If I die before you, would you marry again?

Wife: Errr…probably, yes.

Husband: Well, I wouldn't want you to be lonely, honey. Do you think you two would live right here, in our house?

Wife: This is a great house. Lots of garage space, lots of tools. Yep, we would live here.

Husband: Would you let him sleep in our bed as well?

Wife: Why not? It is soooo comfy.

Husband: Would you even let him wear my car club T-Shirts and use my tools and the lift in my garage?

Wife : Why waste that stuff, it's useful!

Husband: How about my two 1955 Fords? Would you let him drive those, too?

Wife: Definitely not! I'll sell those. He is a Chevy guy.

APOLOGY

Two Chevy guys and two Ford guys were crossing a rickety-roped suspension bridge over a deep mountain gorge, when the rope broke on the far end. All four guys were hanging onto a single rope down the side of the ravine, and the rope seemed to be giving way under the weight. They realized that two of them would have to volunteer to let go, in order to save the other two. After a minute, the two Ford guys exclaimed that they had been wrong all their lives, and that

Chevies were the best-looking and fastest cars in the world. Their final words of apology deeply touched the two Chevy guys, and they responded by clapping...

PARTY LOYALTY TEST

It was election season and a party volunteer was visiting all the houses in town. A small kid answered the door. "Tell me, young man," said the politician, "Is your daddy an independent guy, a Republican guy or a Democrat?" "Neither," said the little boy, "he's a Chevy guy."

CAR TIME

A car show was being held at 1:30 p.m. sharp at an elegant estate with an entrance gate. Attendees had to stop at the gate first and then speak into a mike at the gate before the gate would open. A driver spoke into the mike and asked: "What time is it?" Security responded: "What kind of car are you driving?" The driver replied: "What difference does it make?" Security replied, "It makes a lot of difference. If you are driving a Ford, it is 1:30 in the afternoon. If you have a military vehicle, it is 1330 hours. If it is a Jaguar, it's 180 minutes to happy hour. If it's a Yugo, the little hand is on the one and the big hand is on the six."

SCOTSMAN IS 1/16TH CHEROKEE

A classic 1952 Studebaker Scotsman was T-boned at a stop sign by a Jeep Cherokee. The body shop was unable to remove all the Cherokee shrapnel, so the Studebaker is now 1/16th Cherokee, and qualifies for Federal benefits including its own casino.

IQ TEST

A popular bar had a new robotic bartender installed. A fellow came in for a drink and the robot asked him, "What's your IQ?" The man replied, "150". So the robot proceeded to make conversation about Ford engineering, quantum physics applied to camshafts, atomic chemistry applied to gas atomization in EFI turbo-charged engines, etc. The man listened intently and thought, "This is really cool." The man decided to test the robot. He left the bar, turned around, and returned for a second drink. Again, the robot asked him, "What's your IQ?" The man responded, "100". So the robot started talking about Y-block engines, big block 390s, C-4 and C-6 transmissions and the like. The man thought to himself, "Wow, this *IS* really cool." The man left but came back for a third time. As before, the robot asked him, "What's your IQ?" The man replied, "50." The robot then said, "So, how's your old Yugo runnin'?"

TAKING CANDY

A ten-year-old boy was walking down the road when a car pulled over next to him. "If you get in the car," the driver says, "I'll give you $10 and a piece of candy." The boy refused and kept on walking. A few moments later, the man driving the car pulled over again. "How about $20 and two pieces of candy?" The kid told the guy to leave him alone and walked on. Still further down the road the man pulled over to the side road. "OK", the man says, "this is my final offer. I'll give you $100 and all the candy you can eat." The ten-year-old boy stops, walks to the car and leans in. "Look Dad," he says to the driver, "You bought the crummy Yugo, Dad. You'll have to live with it!"

CHEVIES ARE MORE BETTER

A Ford guy and a Chevy guy were arguing about which was more better. The Ford guy was from Texas. The Ford guy grinned wide and said, "Buddy, you don't cotton to how we do things in Texas. In Texas, we settle small disagreements like this with the Texas Two-Punch Rule." The Chevy guy asked, "What is the Texas Two-Punch Rule?" The Ford guy replied, "Well, first I punch you two times and then you punch me twice. And so on, until someone caves in and admits that the other guy was more right." The Chevy guy decided to try the Texas Two-Punch Rule. The Ford guy walked up to the Chevy guy. The first punch in the gut dropped the Chevy guy to his knees. The second punch in the kidney doubled him over. The Chevy guy collected himself and said: "Okay, you dumb Ford nut, now it's my turn." The Ford guy just smiled and walked away, saying, "Naw, I give up. Chevies are more better than Fords after all."

LUCAS

Q: Why do the British drink warm beer at their car shows?

A: Because Lucas Electronics makes their refrigerators! (And also electronics for their cars).

ANOTHER LUCAS

Q: Why do British cars drive with their headlights off?

A: Because of Lucas, Prince of Darkness!

BRITISH TRIUMPH

Q: Why did the cat sleep under the British Triumph?

A: Because he wanted to wake up oily. (Early...get it?)

HEATED TAILGATES

Q: Why do they fit heated tailgates to luxury Dodge trucks?

A: To keep your hands warm when you push them!

FREE DOG

Q. Why are Daewoo dealers giving away a dog with each Daewoo sold?

A: So the owner has a companion to walk home with.

OLD VOLKSWAGEN'S GO...

Q. Where do Volkswagens go when they get old?

A. The Old Volks home.

RUSSIAN LADA

Q: What's the difference between a golf ball and a Russian Lada?

A: A golf ball can be driven 300 yards. (Not the Lada...)

USER'S MANUAL

Q: What is on page 3 of the Hyundai Owner's Manual?

A: The phone numbers for Uber and Lyft.

YUGO CHALLENGE

Q: What do you call a Yugo at the top of a steep hill?

A: A miracle!

CAR JOKE

Q: Want to hear a car joke?

A: Chevy Chevette!

PATTY CRASHED 454 MONTE CARLO

Tom: My wife Patty just crashed my 1970 Chevy 454 Monte Carlo.

Bay City Bob: Wow, is she OK?

Tom: She will need a new left front fender and some paint and buffing, but she will be alright.

JAMES' PROMISE

James was an eighteen-year-old athletic swimmer in his final year of high school. He went unshaved at the beginning of the year and grew long hair, a beard, and a moustache. It was scruffy and unruly. His Mom hated it. So she promised him that if he got all A's in his last semester and shaved off his gorilla-looking facial hair, she would buy him a new Camaro to use in his freshman year in college. James worked hard and got all A's. He said to his Mom: "I got all A's Mom, now do I get the Camaro? "Not until you shave your gorilla face" she said. "But," James pleaded, "I got all A's. And besides, Jesus had a full beard and moustache." His Mom shot back: "Yes, but Jesus walked most everywhere and sometimes rode a donkey."

FORD VS. CHEVY

Did you know CHEVY is an acronym? Ford guys spell it out as: Cannot Have Expensive Vehicle Yet.

Chevy Guys spell out Ford: Fixed Or Repaired Daily.

BEST ACRONYMS FOR POPULAR AMERICAN CARS

BUICK – Big Untamed Import Car Killer

BUICK - Built Under Industrial Cannibal Kinfolk

DODGE – Drains Or Drops Grease Everywhere

DODGE - Dear Old Dads Get Excited

DODGE - Dwarfs Overseas Deadwood Garbage Easily

FORD – First On Rust and Deterioration

FORD - Fast On Rutted Desert

FORD - Found on Road Dead

FORD - First on Racing Domain

FORD - First On Race Day

JEEP – Just Eats Every Penny

JEEP - Just Expect Every Problem

JEEP - Just Empty Every Pocket

JEEP - Jolts Every Excited Psyche

JEEP – Jeeps Endanger Earnest Passengers

JEEP – Joyride Excites Extroverted Personalities

JEEP - Junkies Expect Ecstatic Pastimes

JEEP - Juveniles Exploring Exotic Pulsations

Sources for above acronyms include:

http://www.careofcars.com/145/funny-car-acronym-for-each-brand/ By Ionut Pavelescu;

http://www.jokes4us.com/miscellaneous jokes/corporatejokes/fordjokes.html;

https://acronyms,thefreedictionary.com/FORD;

https://www.allacronyms.com/DODGE;

https://jalopnik.com/the-definitive-guide-to-derogatory-auto-acronyms-5879789;

https://www.abbreviations.com/CHEVY;

http://www.lotsofjokes.com/car_acronyms.asp;

https://upjoke.com/mustang-jokes;

http://www.careofcars.com/145/funny-car-acronym-for-each-band/;

https://www.tapatalk.com/groups/norcal_drift/the-full-list-of-car-acronyms-t481.html

This author has created new acronyms for a comprehensive list of other cars. Here they are alphabetically. Enjoy them or create your own!

AUTHOR'S ACRONYMS FOR 59 OTHER CARS

ACURA – Asia's Curse Upon Rotund Americans

ACURA - All Cars Uncork Regurgitated Antipathy

ALFA-ROMERO – All Loosely Fitted Accessories Remain On Motorway Ensnaring Oldsters

ASTON MARTIN – Anglophiles Seek To Own; Not Many Are Really Truly Insanely Nimble

AUDI – Accelerates Under Drunken Influence

BENTLEY – British Excess Needs To Liberate Every Yokel

BMW – Bring Many Women

BMW - Big Moola Wasted

BUGATTI – Bug Unlimited; Grates And Terrifies The Ignorant

CADILLAC – Cowboys And Doctors Insist Ladies Love American Cars

CHEVROLET – Customers Hate Endless Varieties; Oddball Lunacy Excites Twits

CITROEN – Caution In Traffic, Tranquil Relaxed Outcast Excites Numskulls

CHRYSLER – Company Has Recalled Your Shrapnel Loser Engine Respectfully

DESOTO – Driven Extinct So Orphans Talk Old-fashioned

DAEWOO – Dadburned Asian Engineering Wastes Our Oil

FERRARI – Fabled Expensive Racer Ravages American Roads Incessantly

FIAT – Feeble Italian Automotive Trouble

GMC – Good Mechanic Called

HENRY J – Hardy Elfish Nerdy Runabout, Yokel's Jalopy

HOLDEN – Humble Old Laughable Drudge Endangered Now

HONDA – Has Ordinary Nerdy Dainty Attributes

HUDSON – Huge Unusual Dazzler Stepsdown On Numskulls

HUMMER – Hairy Uncouth Manly Machine Exudes Ruggedness

HYUNDAI – Henpecked Yuppies Use Noisy Daffy Aberrant Import

ISUZU – Imagine Something Ugly Zipping Urgently

JAGUAR – Jazzy Acceleration Gets Underwear Raunchy

KAISER – Kinky American Invention Shook Every Road

KIA – Korea's Idiotic Aberration

LADA – Laughable Absurd Dumpy Auto

LAMBORGHINI – Leadsled Always Maintains Big Overblown Recycled Gadgetry; Hardly Inflates Nameplates Image

LINCOLN – Luxury In Nice Colors Only Likes Nobility

LOTUS – Loads Of Trouble, Usually Serious

MASERATI – Might Arrange Strong Extra Rope And Towing Implements

MAYBACH – Mercedes Achieves Yacht Behemoth And Creates Havoc

MAZDA – Made After Zero Design Attempts

MERCEDES – Most Expensive Relaxing Car Earnestly Driven, Enhances Superrich

MERCURY – Macho Engines Rankle Carbuncles, Unsightly Rattling Yachts

MINI – Munchkin Imitating Nimble Insect

MITSUBISHI – Mutations Include Turbos; Shudders Until Backfire Is Seriously Hostile Inside

MORGAN – Muddled Outdated Rattletrap: Almost Neanderthal

NASH – Nerdy Antique Sooo Homely

NISSAN – Note I Say Something About Nothing

OLDSMOBILE – Old Loafers Driving Slowly Make Others Incessantly Late Everyday

PACKARD – Proper Antique Classic, King Achieves Respectable Devotion

PEUGEOT – Parisians Endanger Uncounted Gremlins Enthused On Technology

PONTIAC – Paunchy Ordinary Noisy Tug In Auto Camouflage

PORSCHE – Proof Outrageously Rich Spoiled Children Have Everything

RENAULT – Really Eccentric Nuts Unfortunately Use Legal Tender

ROLLS – Respectable Outrageous Leisurely Luxury Sedan

SAAB – Swedish Antiques Always Bedazzle

SKODA – Silly Kooky Offbeat Decadent Auto

SMART – Small Mini Accepts Really Trim

STUDEBAKER – Sensible Thrifty Unfortunate Dictator* Emerged Backwards After Keeping Expectations Rakish (*there was a Studebaker dictator in the late 1930's but the model name was dropped after the rise of Hitler and Mussolini.)

SUZUKI – Squeaky Unstable Zany Uncouth Kimono Immigrant

SUBARU -Screwed Up Blooper Amuses, Rattles, Unloved

TESLA – Technologically Exceptional Sedan Looks Adorable

TOYOTA – Thrifty Old Yanks Overvalue This Auto

VOLVO – Voodoo Occult Lunacy Vexes Oddballs

VOLKSWAGEN – Very Offbeat Little Knick-knack Sells Weighty Americans Goofy Eccentric Nutcracker

YUGO – Yugoslavian Useless Goofy Oddity

FORD GUY VS. CHEVY GUYS

Three guys—two Chevy guys and a Ford guy—are walking together one day and find an exotic lantern, and a Genie pops out of it: "You have freed me from the lamp, and I thank you all. I will give you three wishes, that's one wish each." The first Chevy guy says: "I want one of every year Chevy muscle car ever built—327s, 409s, 454s—all those kinds of cars that beat Fords on the drag strip," he says. The Genie blinked and all the muscle cars appeared. The second Chevy guy says: "I want the protection of a huge wall around all those muscle car Chevys, so that none of those dern fool Ford people can come in." Again, with a blink of the Genie's eye, 'POOF' there was a huge wall around all the Chevys. The Ford guy asks the Genie: "Please tell me more about this wall". The Genie explains: "The wall is 150 feet high, 50 feet thick, is waterproof, and completely surrounds all the Chevys, and nothing can get in or out." The Ford guy ponders a moment and then commands the Genie to fulfill the third wish: "Good, fill it up with concrete."

CHAPTER SIX.

IT'S TOOL TIME!

Every auto aficionado loves tools, whether handy with them or not...

TWENTY-TWO TOOLS

CHOPSAW: Turns metal cherry red hot, and the piece which falls off lights your greasy rag on fire.

HACKSAW: Cuts metal in unpredictable directions.

OXYACETYLENE TORCH: Accidentally lights shop rags in your shop on fire.

TWEEZERS: A slim tool to pick metal shavings from your hand.

ENGINE HOIST: A massive creation which is much stronger than the thin bolts which hold your chain to the carburetor intake manifold.

HYDRAULIC FLOOR JACK: Used to raise a car to the highest point, but it's not high enough anyway. Cinder block and a two x six are accessories.

TROUBLE LIGHT: Also called a drop light since it is often dropped shattering the light bulb. Then you are in trouble.

DRILL PRESS: A tall upright tool used to snatch metal off the drill table and fling it to bruise your knuckles and spill your diet ginger ale mixed with vodka.

VICE GRIPS: Used with plyers to round off nuts and create blood blisters.

PORTABLE ELECTRIC DRILL: Drills seatbelt mounting holes in your truck's floor immediately above the gas line.

WIRE WHEEL: Removes fingerprints and also flings parts elsewhere in the garage, never to be seen again.

WHITWORTH SOCKETS: Obsolete British sockets which will never be used but will be saved anyway.

E-Z OUT BOLT EXTRACTOR: Not that E-Z to use and the bolt which comes out can't be used anyway.

½ x 16-INCH SCREWDRIVER: A straight tool too massive to be used as a screwdriver but not massive enough to be used as a pry bar. Makes you look like a macho pro.

PHILLIPS SCREWDRIVER: An alcoholic drink made with vodka and Phillips Milk of Magnesia, used to ease the frustrations of using other tools.

AIR COMPRESSOR: A noisy, expensive machine which leaks compressed air where the hose is split and tightly taped. Also, leaks where it connects to the tire gauge and where the gauge fits over the nozzle on the tire valve.

HOSE CUTTER: A scissors-like tool used to cut the wrong hoses first.

JACKKNIFE: After breaking a thumbnail to open, blade is found too dull to cut anything. A half hour spent looking for a lost wet stone.

TABLE SAW: Screaming scary rotating shark's teeth trying to bite your fingers or your push tool.

GASKET SCRAPER: Rarely used to scrape gaskets; often used to scrape dried animal poop off your garage floor.

HAMMER: Blunt instrument used to strike the unintended adjacent part, which is now ruined.

ALLEN KEY: A hexagonal steel shaft needed to turn an allen screw, but the screw size is indeterminable as "Metric" or "SAE", so you never have the correct size anyway.

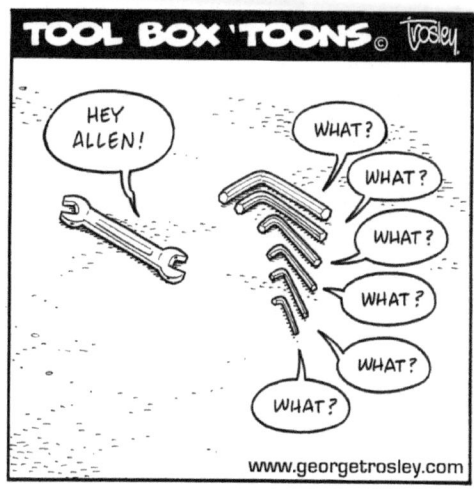

MORE TOOL JOKES FOLLOW

DEALING WITH TRAUMA

Q: Which tool best handles traumatic events?

A: A coping saw!

BAD TRIP

Hippie high on grass to girlfriend: "Imagine that you're stuck in a locked car, sinking in the river, with no windows, no key, no power doors, all locked. How do you solve this problem?"

Girlfriend: "You stop imagining it!"

UNLOVED?

Q. Did you hear about the unhappy mechanic whose wife divorced him because of his love for expensive power tools?

A. At least his saw reciprocated.

BUILDER A FEW SCREWS SHORT

A man went to a tool store to buy a chainsaw so he could cut trees to build a garage for his cars. The salesman sells him the top-of-the-line model, saying that it will cut through over 100 trees in one day. The man takes the chainsaw home and begins working on the trees, but after working for hours he only cuts down two trees. "How can I cut for hours and hours and only take down two trees?" he asks himself. The man brings the chainsaw back to the store and complains that it doesn't work right. "It looks okay," says the salesman, as he starts up the chainsaw, which putt-putts happily. The man jumps back in shock and says, "Wow, what's all that noise?"

MECHANIC WHO FELL

Did you hear about the mechanic who fell onto his running sawz-all?

It was a gut-wrenching experience!

LONELY DRILL

Q. Why wasn't the drill ever invited to parties?

A. Because it's a boring tool.

STUMPED ENGINEERS

Four engineers get into a car but it won't start. The mechanical engineer states: "The engine must be stuck! Someone get me my tool kit." The chemical engineer then says: "No, no, the fuel has ethanol and has water in it." The electrical engineer speaks up: "Both of you are mistaken. There is a short in the electrical system. Lastly, the computer engineer thinks he has the solution: "Listen you fellows. Before you start taking the car apart, let's get out, get back in, and try to restart it."

DULL MECHANIC

Have you heard about the assembly-line mechanic who only honed out the cylinders rebuilding engines? He liked to talk about his work but it was mostly boring.

POPE'S FAVORITE

What's the Pope's favorite power tool?

A cathedrill! *(Groan)*

CAR REPAIR RULES

1. Always use the perfect tool on your car.

2. The perfect tool is usually a hammer.

3. Most tools can be used as a hammer.

WIFE'S COMPLAINT

My husband keeps borrowing my kitchen utensils and using them in the garage, even though he knows it upsets me. He says it's a whisk he's willing to take. *(Groan).*

(The previous eleven jokes adapted from www.upjoke.com/tool-jokes)

OOPS!

A young fellow had way too many informal street races under his belt when Judge Ironsides sentenced him to two years in prison. Fortunately, he was a motor head and wound up in the prison machine shop. He resolved never again to get in trouble, and he got out after 14 months with good behavior. He decided to never tell anyone that he had been in prison. He quickly got a job in a machine shop, and asked out a young lady for a date. He went to pick her up, and she said: "Let's go in my brand new Mustang". He said fine, and as she opened the garage door, he noticed her new license plate. The vanity tag rung a bell in his head: "GIDDY UP". He blurted out to his date: "Hey. Guess what? I made that license plate!" (Oops...)

CHAPTER SEVEN

SALUTE TO JEFF FOXWORTHY

With his books, CD's and standup comedy, Jeff Foxworthy has done a stellar job of defining rednecks' personalities, dating habits, lifestyle, quirks, and how they view their autos.

Jeff Foxworthy is the top-selling comedy artist ever, A Grammy Award nominee, and a best-selling author of 26 books. He has defined the "Redneck" every which way but loose in his books, live comedy acts, CD's, the Blue Collar Comedy tour movies, Comedy Central TV, and a weekly radio show "The Foxworthy Countdown". He hosts the Fox TV series "Are You Smarter than a 5th Grader". He sells everything including T-Shirts, mugs, and sportswear on his website http://www.jefffoxworthy. com/. Many car club newsletters and emails circulated among car aficionados include his jokes.

First, this chapter is ONLY focused on how rednecks deal with their autos. Second, we must lay out Foxworthy's view of "Rednecks" in order to contrast them with the author's view of a different animal—the "Good Ol' Boy" which this author has conceptualized in auto-related humor.

Here is a big batch of Jeff's Redneck auto-related definitions. The selection of items is rearranged by this author and not by Jeff Foxworthy. These joke titles are the author's, not Jeff Foxworthy's. After this chapter, the author's new concept of "Good Ol' Boy" appears in Chapter 8. I think that Foxworthy's rednecks and Placek's good ol' boys would get along fine and be good friends.

JEFF FOXWORTHY SAYS "TEN HINTS YOU ARE A REDNECK"

"1. You've ever rebuilt a transmission in your bathtub.

2. You buy lots of kitty litter but you do not own a cat.

3. You don't care if your radio works because you'd rather listen to the sounds from the engine.

4. Your garage has more square footage than your house.

5. You've memorized your car's VIN # but you can't remember your own phone number.

6. You have a tattoo of your first car somewhere on your body.

7. You once had a drag race to defend your sister's honor.

8. Your emergency room doctor asks your blood type and you reply "10W40".

9. Your favorite junk yard calls you whenever something "good" comes in.

10. You really like the small of citrus hand cleaner...and you use it after you shower."

STILL TEN MORE WAYS TO ID A REDNECK, SAYS FOXWORTHY

"1. After making love you ask your date to roll down the window.

2. You have flowers planted in a car part in your front yard.

3. There are two or more cars up on blocks in the front yard.

4. Your vehicle has a two-tone paint job--primer red and primer gray.

5. Your mom calls you over to help, because she has a flat tire...on her house.

6. You have spent more on your pickup truck than on your education.

7. You have a color-coordinating rope that ties down your car hood.

8. You replace a flat tire on your truck with a tire from your house.

9. Your truck has more in it when you come home from the garbage dump with more than you went with.

10. Your kitchen table has more grease on it than your engine does."

FOXWORTHY HAS YET ANOTHER TEN TIPS ON REDNECKS

"1. You prefer car keys to Q-Tips.

2. You go to a stock car race and don't need a program.

3. You see no need to stop at a rest stop 'cause you have an empty milk jug in the car.

4. You have a rag for a gas cap.

5. Your home has more miles on it than your car.

6. Fewer than half of your cars run.

7. The rear tires on your car are at least twice as wide as the front ones.

8. You have a Hefty bag on the passenger side window of your car.

9. You own at least 20 hats with truck logos.

10. You consider your license plate personalized because your dad made it in prison."

WASN'T IT FOXWORTHY WHO SAID YOU NEED NEW WHEELS WHEN...?

"1. You lose the stoplight challenge to a 14-year-old on a moped...

2. 15-minute Jiffy Lube needs to keep your car for 3 days...

3. You keep losing passengers on left turns...

4. Your tires are balding faster than Telly Savalas...

5. The engine burns more oil than gas...

6. You judge suitable parking spaces by the degree of downhill slope...

7. You have the local tow company on speed-dial...

8. The engine catches fire and you don't notice anything wrong until the firetruck pulls you over...

9. You can leave your car parked, unlocked, with the keys in the ignition, and not worry about it being stolen...

10. Public transportation starts to look good..."

WOW, MORE JEFF!

Jeff Foxworthy says you might be a Redneck if...

"1. You've ever experienced road range in your own driveway.

2. You think the last four words of the National Anthem are "Gentlemen, start your engines."

3. There's a hole in the ozone layer directly above your house.

4. The hardest part of your divorce was dividing up your license plate collection.

5. You keep getting hurt falling off your truck seat because your truck has a 15" lift job.

6. Your entire car isn't worth the minimum insurance deductible."

TEN MORE TIPS THAT YOU MIGHT BE A REDNECK BY JEFF FOXWORTHY

"1. You ever cut your grass and found a car.

2. You own a home that is mobile and five cars that aren't.

3. Your stereo speakers used to belong to the drive-in theater.

4. You read the Auto Trader with a highlight pen.

5. You've totaled every car you've ever owned.

6. The taillight covers of your car are covered with red tape.

7. Your kids take a siphon hose to "Show and Tell."

8. People hear your car a long time before they see it.

9. The gas pedal on your car is shaped like a bare foot.

10. You once sold a car for gas money."

AND FINALLY TWO THINGS THAT A REDNECK WILL NEVER SAY...

"1. Who's Richard Petty?

2. The tires on that truck are too big."

(Jokes by Foxworthy can be found everywhere, including: www.gameboomers.com; www.onelinerz. net; www.forum.burek.com; www.crosskit.com; www.countryhumor.com; www.imgur.com; www. hotredneakwomaninokla.blog; www.sangre-de-cristo.com; www.wilk4.com; www.getamused.com; www.dennydavis.net; www.scale4x4sc.org; www.pacoenterprisesblogspot.com; www.issuu.com;www. cartalk.com).

CHAPTER EIGHT

GOOD OL' BOYS DEFINED

Jeff Foxworthy has described The American "Redneck". I, however, will describe an alternate creature, the American "Good Ol' Boy". Please see three illustrations of the Good Ol' Boy as depicted by the illustrator, Shelby Rehn.

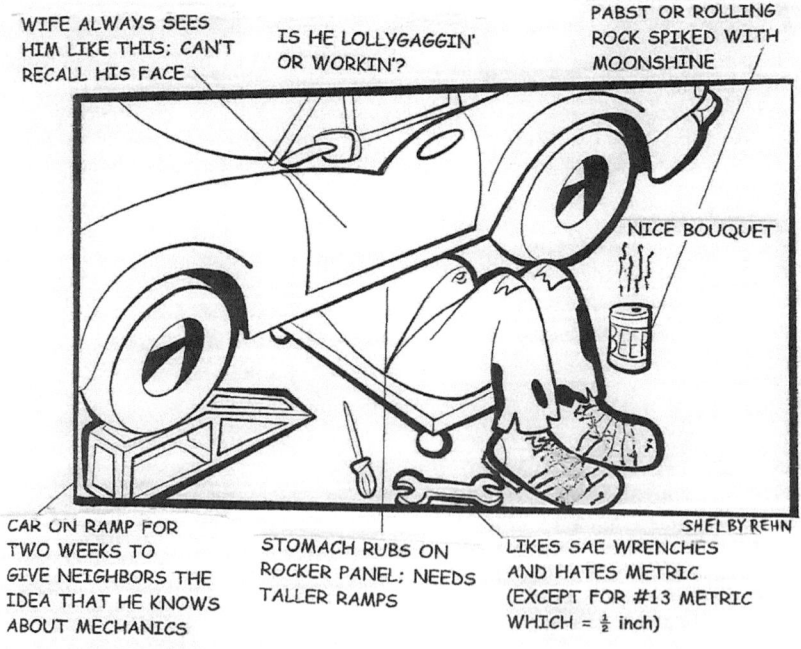

WIFE ALWAYS SEES HIM LIKE THIS; CAN'T RECALL HIS FACE

IS HE LOLLYGAGGIN' OR WORKIN'?

PABST OR ROLLING ROCK SPIKED WITH MOONSHINE

NICE BOUQUET

BEER

CAR ON RAMP FOR TWO WEEKS TO GIVE NEIGHBORS THE IDEA THAT HE KNOWS ABOUT MECHANICS

STOMACH RUBS ON ROCKER PANEL; NEEDS TALLER RAMPS

LIKES SAE WRENCHES AND HATES METRIC (EXCEPT FOR #13 METRIC WHICH = $\frac{1}{2}$ inch)

SHELBY REHN

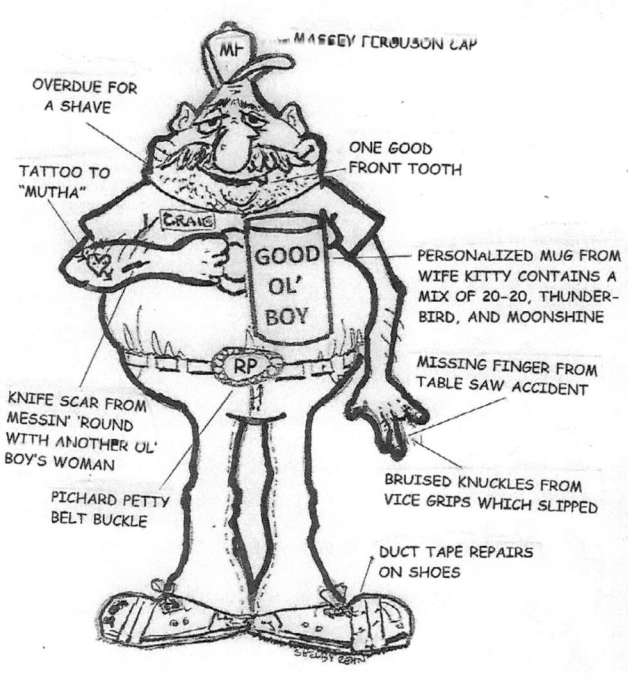

MASSEY FERGUSON CAP

OVERDUE FOR A SHAVE

ONE GOOD FRONT TOOTH

TATTOO TO "MUTHA"

PERSONALIZED MUG FROM WIFE KITTY CONTAINS A MIX OF 20-20, THUNDER-BIRD, AND MOONSHINE

MISSING FINGER FROM TABLE SAW ACCIDENT

KNIFE SCAR FROM MESSIN' 'ROUND WITH ANOTHER OL' BOY'S WOMAN

PICHARD PETTY BELT BUCKLE

BRUISED KNUCKLES FROM VICE GRIPS WHICH SLIPPED

DUCT TAPE REPAIRS ON SHOES

GOOD OL' BOY

REFLECTION OFF SHINY BALD HEAD ADDS LIGHT TO DARK GARAGE

EYEBROWS SINGED OFF WHEN CARBURETOR BACK-FIRED WHILE SPRAYING QUICKSTART ETHER

BRAIN THINKS ALL GOOD INVENTIONS CAME FROM DETROIT

HAS NOT SEEN HIS FACE IN 10 YEARS

BROKEN TEETH FROM HOLDING TOOLS IN MOUTH

HIS LAST CAN OF BILLY BEER FROM WHEN JIMMY CARTER WAS PRESI-DENT IN 1977

SALVAGED WESTERN AUTO SHIRT FROM RAG DISGARD PILE

SPOTS ON WHITE DOG ARE USED OIL

CAR ON HYDRAULIC JACK TO INSTALL PORTO-WALLS OVER BLACKWALLS

USED MOTOR OIL FROM BENDING OVER OIL PAN

HEAVY GREASE BETWEEN TOES

DOG'S NAME IS "MAVERICK"

PAUL J. PLACEK, PH.D.

DESCRIPTION OF GOOD OL' BOYS

"Good Ol' Boys" drive all kinds of vehicles and can be from any region of the country, but they do tend to live in small towns or out in the country (hardly ever in the big city). "Good Ol' Boys" tend to drink beer, often at the "watering hole".

"Good Ol' Boys" are more likely than "Rednecks" to use certain figures of speech. They may drag out the length of certain words (which sounds downright lovely when spoken by a Southern Belle). "Good Ol' Boys" use the word "rightly" to replace the word "exactly"—e.g., "I don't rightly know", ""perty" for "pretty", and "pert' near" for "almost". "Good Ol' Boys" more often say: "et" (for "ate"), "blew up the motor" (for a broken engine), "Lord willin' and the creek don't rise" (for, "if at all possible"), and "lollygaggin'" (for laying around, doing nothing). Good ol' boys say "pick 'em up truck" (for pickup truck). They say "his 'un'" (for his own), "her 'un " (for her own), "their 'un" (for their own), "we'uns" (for we all), and "your 'un" (for your own). Good ol' boys say "chip off the old block" (a son is like his father), "tom cattin' around" (a male chasing after many females), "disremember" (i.e., forget), and "got her in a family way" (impregnated her). Good ol' boys say "taar" for tire and "flares" for flowers. "Fearsome" means "afraid of". Everything I say is a true fer certin' fact, at least until the Fed'ral guv 'mint spends 10 million clams on a national survey to prove me plug fer shure wrong.

(Grammar adapted from www.http:/www.grammer.yourdictionary.com/slang/American-slang-dictionary)

THE DUKES OF HAZZARD

Good ol' boys were partially defined in the TV series "The Dukes of Hazzard", a comedy-action CBS show which aired from 1979 to 1985. Waylon Jennings was the balladeer who wrote and sang the theme song, "Good Ol' Boys." He described the antics of Bo and Luke, who drove a 1969 Dodge Charger with a Confederate flag on top. The politically-correct folks do not like the fact that the Confederate flag was on top, but might take satisfaction that 150 Confederate-flagged Chargers were destroyed in the 145 episodes. Other characters were Rosco, Daisy, Cooter, Cletus, and Enos.

The Dukes of Hazzard "Good Ol' Boys" theme song was written and performed by Waylon Jennings. The lyrics follow:

"Just the good ol' boys

Never meanin' no harm

Beats all you never saw

Been in trouble with the law
Since the day they was born

Staightenin' the curves

Flattenin' the hills

Someday the mountain might get 'em
But the law never will

Makin' their way

The only way they know how

That's just a little bit more
Than the law will allow

Makin' their way

The only way they know how yeah

That's just a little bit more
Than the law will allow

I'm a good ol' boy

You know my momma loves me

But she don't understand
They keep a showin' my hands

And not my face on TV"

(http://www.imdb.com; www.azlyricsondemand.com)

ANOTHER VERSION OF "GOOD OL' BOYS"

There is a different version called "Just Good Ol' Boys "written by Ansley Fleetwood, a novelty-single released in 1979 sung by Moe Bandy and Joe Stampley. It gives more complete descriptions of exaggerated good ol' boy behaviors than the Waylon Jennings song. It was a number one hit.

JUST GOOD OL' BOYS"

Well, I've been kicked out of might near every bar around

I've been locked up for drivin' a hundred and twenty through town

Well, I've been shot at and cut with a knife

For messing 'round with another man's wife

But other than that we ain't nothing, just good ol' boys...

I threw my boss out a window and got fired from my last job

Hot-wired a city truck and turned it over in the Mayor's yard

Well I beat my brother-in-law half to death

I lost twenty bucks on his football bet

But other than that we ain't nothing, just good ol' boys...

Good ol' boys, we're all the same

Ain't no way we'll ever change

Mean no harm by the things we do

Or the trouble that we get into

Other than a wild hare once in a while

We can't help it, it's just our style

And good ol' boys is all we'll ever be...

I got an alimony payment that's six weeks overdue

I got caught with a trunk full of bootleg out-a-state booze

I hocked my wife's diamond ring last June

Bought me an outboard Evinrude

But other than that we ain't nothin', just good ol' boys...

Good ol' boys, we're all the same

Ain't no way we'll ever change

Mean no harm by the things we do

Or the trouble that we get into

Other than a wild hare once in a while

We can't help it, it's just our style

Good ol' boys is all we'll ever be

Good ol' boys is all we'll ever be"

(https://www.classic-county-song-lyrics.com; https://en.wikipedia.org; https://www.imdb.com;

https://www.warnerbros.com; https://www.mentalfloss.com)

Now you, as a true student of American culture, understand the difference between a "redneck" and a "good ol' boy". A "redneck" has been thoroughly described by Jeff Foxworthy. However, a "good ol' boy" will now be further described in my humorous jokes in this book. The author will humbly accept all accolades, which are well-deserved. The accolades will endure until a multi-million dollar Federal survey proves me wrong. Now for some of the author's good ol' boy humor...

TRAILER-LESS GOOD OL' BOYS

Did you hear that the Governor's Mansion and surrounding neighborhood in Richmond, Virginia burned down? Yep. Pert' near took out the whole trailer park, making many good ol' boys homeless.

GOOD OL' BOY RULE

Anytime you have a 50-50 chance of getting something right, there's a 90% probability you'll get it wrong. That is, Lord willin' and the creek don't rise.

GOOD OL' BOY WISDOM

Every good ol' boy must rightly know two things: How to jump a battery and how to push-start a car.

GOOD OL' BOY REPAIRS

For every good ol' boy car repair action, there is a puzzling, rattling, screeching opposite reaction. It often ends in a blown up motor.

GOOD OL' BOYS BEAR LEFT

Two good ol' boys were in the woods, driving down a dirt road in an old truck. They saw a sign with an arrow that read "BEAR LEFT". Fearsome of bears, they quick made a U-turn and skedaddled home.

GOOD OL' BOYS AND BONDS

Q. What is the difference between good ol' boys and government bonds?

A. The bonds mature.

GOOD OL' BOYS AND READING

Q. How many good ol' boys does it take to read the directions before installing a car part?

A. We'uns don't know; it has not never happened.

FLAT TARR

There was this good ol' boy from Alabama who had a flat tire. He got out of his pickup, lucked into a patch of wildflowers, and picked some. He tied some on his front bumper, and some to his back bumper. A biker drove by and saw the truck with flowers and asked the ol' boy what the problem was. The ol' boy replied, "I plum fer sure got a flat tarr." The biker asked: "Why the flowers?" The good ol' boy responded: "When you have a flat tarr, they tell ya' to put flares in the front and flares in the back! It works, but I'll never not know why."

TEN GOOD OL' BOY RULES FER RIDIN' SHOTGUN*

(*The front passenger seat, so named after the guard's seat on the stagecoach in the Wild West.)

1. Yall 'uns don't fer sure need to tote a real shotgun (less'n y'all in the big city).

2. The dude what holds the pink slip (title) always gits first dibs on riding shotgun.

3. The main squeeze of the owner don't need to claim shotgun; batting her eyes at the owner will do.

4. If shotgun ain't called, the right front seat goes to whoever has the most urgent business (sech as deliverin' papers, whackin' mailboxes, headin' for the porto-potty, or cruisin' for chicks.)

5. If the shotgun seat is up for grabs, whoever shouts "shotgun!" first gits it, providin' the car is in sight and no one has opened the door yet.

6. If the owner is liquor-impaired or blotto, he is offered shotgun.

7. If a rear seat rider's stomach is roiled such that he might toss his cookies, he may be required to ride shotgun with his window open in order to keep the inside of the car sanitary.

8. If only one person knows how to read, or can understand a map, or can program a GPS, he gets shotgun.

9. If the owner is big or strong or fit or sober, he may require a free-for-all fistfight to get shotgun, sech that he feels superior to the others when he wins. (Useful if members of the fair sex are present).

10. No one who is "un-cool" may ride shotgun, least the vehicle itself be disgraced.

(Note: The author used the generic "he" in these rules, but sturdy farm gals, ladies wearing cowgirl hats and boots, impaired sorority girls, and soiled doves may insert "she" as appropriate.)

THINGS GOOD OL' BOYS DON'T SAY

1. Duct tape won't not never fix that.

2. Honey, I think we should sell the pick 'em up and buy an SUV.

3. No dad-berned kids in the bed of the pick 'em up, it just ain't safe.

GOOD OL' BOY FROM KAHOOTS

A good ol' boy lived in Kahoots with several friends. He had a girlfriend in Cognito, where no one recognized him. His ex-wife lived in Sane, where his children would drive him. As he got older, he always wanted to go to Conclusions, but you have to jump to get there, and he was too old to jump. He had been in Doubt, but he wondered why he went there, so he left. He had been in Flexible, but people there were too rigid. He had also been in Capable, and he had no idea how he got home. When he went to get his motor fixed he liked to be in Suspense, but he never knew if it would start afterwards. In the end, he got lost, in Continent, where it was wet and damp. And THAT'S what happens to good ol' boys in the end, plum shure fer certin'.

DADDY AND DARLA

A good ol' boy and his little eight-year-old daughter Darla walked into a dentist's office. The man said to the dentist: "Doc, we're in one heck of a hurry since we are goin' to go to a car show, we don't have no time for your Novocain shot to get the gums numb. I just want you to pull the tooth, and be done with it! We have a 10:00 a.m. show time and its 9:30 already...we don't even have no time to wait for the anesthetic to work!" The dentist thought to himself, "What a brave guy and dedicated car enthusiast." So the dentist asks him, "Which tooth is it, sir?" The man looked his little daughter and said, "Open yer mouth Darla, and show him..."

MOLOTOV GOOD OL' BOY

Q. What did the enemy do when a good ol' boy soldier threw a quart jar full gasoline with a cloth wick sticking out?

A. They just lit the wick and threw it back.

AM/PM

Q: Did you hear about the good ol' boy who bought a 1970 Mustang which had an A.M. radio?

A: He never did figure out that he could also play it at night.

SMART OL' BOY?

One day, Jimmy was walking down Main Street when he saw his friend Bubba driving a beautiful red '56 Sunliner. Bubba pulled up to him with a wide grin.

Jimmy said: "Bubba, where'd you get that plum-beautiful ragtop?"

"Tammie give it to me," ol' boy Bubba proudly replied.

Jimmy said: "I knew she was kinda sweet on ya', but a bodacious perty convertible?"

Bubba said: "Tammy picked me up in this red ragtop. We'uns was driving down a country road, and then Tammy pulled off the road and drove down this wooded trail deep into the woods where there was no one else around. She parked the car, got out a blanket, pitched all her clothes off, lay down plum necked and said ever so sweetly: "Bubba, take whatever you'un want."

Bubba says: "So I fired up that 312 Y-Block in that ragtop and drove off!" Jimmy thought and said: "And you wouldn't a fit in her clothes neither."

FORGETFUL

Good ol' boys Homer and Jethro were two old guys who liked to work on their antique cars. They were getting very forgetful, and both were told by their doctor that they are physically OK, but that they should start writing things down to stop disremembering things. One Saturday morning, Homer was in his garage working under an old car he had jacked up, and he asked Jethro to get him a ½" socket from his truck. "Write it down so you don't forget," Homer told Jethro. "No, I can remember ½" socket," Jethro says. Homer said "Also get me a ratchet wrench with it, and write it down so you don't forget." Jethro walks off toward the tools in his truck and he is irritated as he says "No, I don't need to have it writ' down—a ½" socket and a ratchet wrench." About 15 minutes later, Jethro comes back and slides a plate of bacon and eggs under the car to Homer. Homer stares at the plate for a minute and says, "So quit lollygaggin' around, where is my toast?"

CAR CLUB DUES

Homer wrote a note to the national president of the "Jalopies Unfit for Nice Kinfolk" car club ("JUNK" for short): "This here pitcher of my rat road is blurred becuz the rat moved. I would have enclosed my $20 dues but I see I have already scaled up the envelope."

ZUCCHINI

A good ol' boy had a big garden, and he sometimes shared with his neighbors. But zucchini was hard to get rid of. So he backed his old Ford pick'em up truck to the end of the driveway by the street, and opened the tailgate. On the tailgate he put a fer certin' big box loaded with zucchini, and on top of the box he propped up a big sign that said "FREE". In the morning, he found that same full box of zucchini on the ground. His pick 'em up truck, however, was gone.

OL' BOY'S CHOICE

A good ol' boy won $40,000 in the lottery and wanted a nice mid-50's Ford. He looked at three mild customs and they were all the same price. The first one he looked at was a red '55 Sunliner with red and white interior and a continental kit. The second one was a '56 black and yellow Crown Vic glasstop with vinyl black and yellow interior and cruiser skirts. The third one was a tropical rose and snowshoe white Crown with sissy bars front and back and wire wheels, and electric windows. WHICH ONE DID HE CHOOSE????

(Give up?)

Answer: The one with the friggin' biggest motor, of course!

WATCH BATTERIES INSTALLED

Good ol' boys Skip and his son Lil' Skip drove by a mall and saw a sign: "WATCH BATTERIES INSTALLED--$5." Skip said to Lil' Skip: "Who on earth is stupid enough to pay to see batteries being installed?" "Not me," said Lil' Skip. Then as they drove away from the mall, Skip said to Lil' Skip: "What time is it?" Lil' Skip replied: "I don't rightly know. My friggin' watch stopped and needs a battery."

HAVING A BALL

A good ol' boy goes to car shows regularly, but all his friends tell him his face always looks grizzled and unshaven. So, he goes into the Ruffsdale Barber Shop for a shave and a haircut before the show. He tells Ken "Scissorhands" the barber he can't get all his whiskers off because his cheeks are wrinkled from age. Ken gets two little wooden balls from a cup on the shelf and tells the guy to put them inside his cheeks to spread out the skin when he shaves that part of his face. When he's finished, the ol' boy tells the barber that was fer certin' the cleanest shave he'd had in years, but he accidentally et the little balls and he was very sorry. "What should I do?" he asked the barber. Ken replied: "Just bring them back in a couple of days like everyone else does".

GOOD OL' BOY AT BAD DRIVER'S SCHOOL

A good ol' boy had way too many tickets and many "points" on his driving record, and the judge ordered him to go to Driver's School. The instructor was lecturing about the evils of alcohol and driving while impaired. He put a glass of water on the podium and dropped a worm into the glass, and the worm swam happily. Next, the instructor put a glass of vodka on the table and dropped a worm into it, and the worm writhed in pain, curled up, and died a miserable death. Proud of his lesson, the instructor said to the class: "Now, do you see what this proves?" The good ol' boy stood up from the back of the room and shouted: "Yesh, if you drink vodka, fer sure you will not never get worms!"

DEVOTION

At a car show, two good ol' boys are talking about engines and shining their fenders. One of the guys is about to polish his chrome when he sees a long funeral procession on the road go by. He stops polishing, takes off his cap, closes his eyes, and bows for a moment of prayer. His buddy says: "Wow, that is fer certin' the most thoughtful and touching thing I have ever seed. You truly are a kind feller." The other good ol' boy then replies: "Yeah, well, we was married for 35 years."

STRIP DOWN

A good ol' boy, Butch, went to Carlisle and decided to buy a set of four extra-wide white radials for his old 1956 Desoto. The lovely gal at the register, ready to take his money, said: "Strip down please, facing me." Butch figured it was some new Homeland Security thing, but being law-abiding, he dropped his pants and removed his shirt. A crowd gathered and the gal's face got red as she said: "No, I meant strip down ON YOUR CREDIT CARD!"

WARREN JUNOR'S BIKE RIDE

Good Ol' Boy Warren decided to get some exercise so he pedaled his bike to the liquor store. He got his two favorite wines, Thunderbird and 20-20, put them in the bike basket, and sat on his bike seat for the ride home. Then he thought: "If'n I fall off this here bike, the bottles will break. And, *that*, he thought, is ALCOHOL ABUSE!" So Warren got off his bike and drank it all, so as not to break the wine bottles. It turned out to be a wise decision, because he fell off his bike six times on his ride back home.

OL' BOY AT DEMO DERBY

A guy goes to a demolition derby in Virginia. He notices an empty seat in the front row with perfect viewing position, in the reserved section. As he sits down, he asks the ol' boy sitting next to him, "Scuse me, is anyone sitting here?" The ol' boy replies "Nope. Sit cher self-down." The guy says: "This is bodacious incredible! Who in their right mind would have a great seat like this and not use it?" The ol' boy replies, "Well, achully, the seat belongs to my darlin' wife. She was 'spose to come with me, but she passed away, deader than a doornail. This is the first race she missed since we got hitched in 1967." The guy said: "That's terrible sad. But couldn't you find someone to give her reserved seat to? A relative or close friend?" "Nope," the ol' boy replied, "They're all at her blessed perty fun'ral today."

GOOD OL' BOYS CRUISE-IN ON JULY 4TH

Bubba was a good ol' boy whose extended family was planning a 4th of July cookout at his rural home. Every adult relative brought their favorite dish and favorite fireworks (Roman candles, cherry bombs, ash cans—all fireworks illegal in that state). They arrived in old pick'em up trucks, rusty cars, low riders, and rat rods. Bubba got a call that a police cruiser got word that illegal fireworks were going to be set off. So Bubba tells his eight-year-old son, Bubba Junior to quick gather up all the fireworks and hide them, fast. Bubba Junior did as he was told. Bubba then tells Cousin Barbara Jean to light the gas propane grill and get some burgers ready. "Just turn on the friggin' gas and punch the ignition button," Bubba says. Bubba then pulls Bubba Junior aside, just as the police cruiser arrived, and says: "Whew!" That was fer certin' close! That dude's a police officer, and he almost saw the fireworks. Did you hide them real good?" Bubba Junior replied: "Oh, yeah, nobody will ever think to look in the grill."

FLY U.S. AIRLINES Y'ALL

A good ol' boy from Georgia calls U.S. Airlines. He says there is a national custom car show in California and he asks how long it takes to fly from Savannah to Los Angeles. The airline agent says, "Just a minute..." The ol' boy says, "Theng ya vera much!" and hangs up.

BACK DIRECTLY FROM YONDER FOR MY "MESS A GREENS"

A good ol' boy goes to the farm market to buy collard greens, kale, etc. a mess of greens. He told his wife he would be back "directly", who figured she knew exactly how long "directly" is – as in: "Going to market, be back directly." She told him fer certin' to come back directly and not do no tom cattin' around whilst he's at market.

GOOD OL' BOY AT A REDLIGHT

A good ol' boy went to visit his friend in the big city. At the red-light, he noticed that the stoplight at the intersection beeped when it was OK for pedestrians to cross. "Wassat for?" he asked. A passerby explained to the ol' boy that it signals to blind people when the light is red. The good ol' boy said: "Does they actually let blind folks drive in this here town?"

GOOD OL' BOY WORKERS

A young preacher in the big city was told to go to a small cemetery to preside over a good ol' boy's funeral. He got lost on the way and was terribly late. The hearse was nowhere in sight, and the workmen were already eating lunch. He went to the open grave and found the concrete vault lid already in place. Taking out his book, he read the service, praying for the good ol' boy's soul to flow to heaven where life is fragrant and pure. As the preacher was returning to his car, one of the workmen quietly whispered to another workman: "Maybe we'd better disremember to not tell him that he prayed over a septic tank."

LAST WORDS OF FRED, A GOOD OL' BOY

Fred was a good ol' boy breathing with the help of oxygen. He was detailing his car underneath at a car show. His best friend Jimmy walked over to him and it was clear that Fred was suddenly having trouble breathing. Jimmy immediately called 911 on his cell phone and waited for help. Meanwhile, Fred, under the car, struggled around, and sadly used his last bit of breath to scribble a note, and then he died. Then the ambulance came, but too late. His friend Jimmy was distraught and weeping, and thought it best not to look at the note at that time, so he placed it in Fred's baseball jacket pocket. At Fred's funeral, as Jimmy was finishing Fred's eulogy to those in attendance, Jimmy realized that Fred was wearing the same baseball Jacket that he was wearing when he died. Jimmy said, "You know, Ol' Fred handed me a note just before he died. I haven't looked at it, but knowing Fred, I'm sure there's a word of inspiration there for us all." He opened the note, and read aloud: "Hey Jimmy, it's plug shure fer certin' that yer standin' on my oxygen tube!"

BACKATCHA

A good ol' boy and his wife are lying in bed, annoyed by the next-door neighbor's boom box in his backyard playing rap music, for hours and hours. The ol' boy jumps up out of bed and says, "I had 'nough a 'dis." He goes out of the house and later returned to bed. The wife says: "That lousy rap music is still playing loud, what have you been doing?" The ol' boy says: "I moved 'dat boom box to OUR backyard...now see how HE likes it!"

DEFINITION OF A BOOGER

Only a good ol' boy knows that the term "booger" can be dirt from the nose. Or, "that ol' booger," is a careless driver who pulls out in front of you in the dark and scares the boogers out of you.

ALLIGATOR SHOES

A good ol' southern boy goes into a Louisiana shoe store and asks the price of some alligator shoes. He had never ever had a pair, and he says he wants to look classy at the next jalopyrama car show. "$500," says the salesman. "I plum can't afford that!" says the old boy. "How 'bout a discount?" The salesman tells him they've just come in from Italy, and there's no way he's discounting them. But the old boy won't give up and keeps pestering him to mark them down. Finally, the salesman, exasperated, says, "Look, there an alligator pond a block from here. Just go catch yourself one and you won't have to pay anything." The old boy says, "That's fer certain a bodacious fine idea." After a couple of hours the salesman starts to feel guilty and wonders if maybe the ol' boy got eaten. He walks over to the pond and sees the old boy surrounded by dead alligators on their backs, feet in the air. The good ol' boy looks up and sees the salesman and yells, "Is this here some kind of joke? Are you yankin' my chain? NOT ONE of these dern fool gators has shoes on!"

OVERKILL

Tim the good ol' boy was in his huge backyard with a bulldozer filling in a huge hole when his neighbor peered over the fence: "What are you up to there, Tim?" "My cat died," replied Tim tearfully without looking up, "and I just buried him." The neighbor was concerned, "That's an awfully big hole for a little cat, isn't it?" Tim replied: "That's because yer wife run him over and he stuck to the taar of your car!!!"

DARE DEVIL

Two good ol' boys meet in a bar for a beer. The 7:00 p.m. news is on TV and there is footage of a man about to jump a motorcycle from one skyscraper roof across the street and land on the other skyscraper roof. Ol' boy #1 says, "I bet you $20 he crashes and burns." Ol' boy #2 says, "I will take your bet, I think he will make the jump OK." Minutes later, the biker jumps, misses his landing, crashes and burns. Ol' boy #2 opens his wallet to give ol' boy #1 the $20. Ol' boy #1 says, "I cain't take your money. I cheated. I seen this an hour ago on the 6:00 p.m. news." Ol' boy #2 replies, "Well shoot, I seen it, too. But I didn't think for a plug second he'd do it again."

DELANEY'S GOOD OL' BOYS CAR SHOW

Out in Hopkins, Georgia, the Good Ol' Boys Car Club organized a car show. It was called the "Hayseeds In Cars Kustoms Show", or "HICKS" for short. Delaney was in charge. It included a tour of moonshine stills and a coon hunt. There were also trophies for the best coon dogs. There were giant trophies for trucks, shiny trophies for shiny cars, tiny trophies for rice burners, fake fur fuzzy hats for rat rods and jelly beans for jelly bean cars.

DELANEY'S GOOD OL' BOY CAR SHOW (CONT'D)

Delaney announced in his newsletter that Tuesday is open for setting up the flea market: "There might be some real fleas around, but we're not going to use names here. Folks with fleas know who they are! We are asking all attendees to bathe daily. Local boys like to use tourists for target practice as they skitter across the road, so don't not wear nuthin' that makes you look like a snipe or a tourist. Visit a spell with the hillbillies. Also, you gotta learn to speak "Southern." This will help you fit in better with the locals. War: Metal strands used to hold up tailpipes and mufflers. Fore: Means "prior to" in the South. Gummut: A large institution in Washington, D.C. that consumes taxes at a fearful rate. Flat Out: Means to drive "at maximum speed", or "the mostest." Garntee: Any kind of warranty. Chekatawlfarya?" (Heard by baffled Yankees at service stations in small Southern towns; usage: 'Check that oil for you?') Rek-On: Believe, Think. I garantee all y'all will have a flat out bodacious good time in Hopkins. I rek-on I better close 'afore the gummut gits after me fer one thing or the other." See ya' soon, Delaney

DELANEY'S LAST UPDATE TO HIS PREVIOUS LAST UPDATE

Here is Delaney's last newsletter update: "I'm writing this last update slow because I know some of you can't read fast. We don't live where we did last month. I read in the newspapers that most accidents happen within 20 miles from your home, so we moved. I won't be able to send you the address because the last Georgia family that lived here took the house numbers when they moved so they wouldn't have to change their address. This new place is really nice. It even has a washing machine. I'm not sure it works so well though. Last week I put a load in and pushed the lever down and I haven't seen those clothes since. Or, maybe it was one of those new-fangled toilets? The weather ain't bad here. It only rained twice last week; the first time for three days and the second time for four days. To Paul Placek, about that oversize 3X shirt I was supposed to mail... I thought it would be too heavy to send in the mail with the buttons on, so I cut them off and put them in the pockets. There, that should help save postage. My younger sister had a baby yesterday but I haven't found out what it is yet so I don't know if I'm an aunt or an uncle. My Uncle Ted fell in the whiskey vat last week. Some men tried to pull him out, but he fought them off. We had him cremated and he exploded and then burned very brightly for three days. The preacher said that Uncle Ted always did brighten folks' lives." ---Delaney

FROZEN OL' BOYS

Q: Why did the good ol' boys freeze to death in their car at the drive-in movie theatre?

A: They went to see "Closed for the Winter".

OL' BOY THIEF

Q: Why did the good ol' boy try to steal a police car?

A: He saw "911" on the back and thought it was a Porsche.

NTSA'S BLACKBOX

The National Transportation Safety Administration (NTSA) recently completed a project with automakers to install black boxes in 4-wheel drive pickup trucks. They would record the driver's last five seconds before an accident. They found that, in most cases, the last words of drivers were "oh darn!" or similar expletive. However, for good ol' boys, the last few words were: "Hold my beer honey and watch this".

PIG!

A good ol' boy was driving down a steep graveled mountain road. A pretty lady was driving up the same narrow gravel road. Just as they passed each other, the lady stuck her head out of her window and shouted: "PIG!" The ol' boy knew a man-hater when he saw one, and leaned out his window looking back and shouted: "BITCH!" The ol' boy continued driving down the road, and as he rounded the corner, he collided with a huge feral pig and wrecked his car. *(Men should listen to women more carefully).*

CHAPTER NINE

AUTO AFICIONADOS AND HIGHER POWERS

The Webster dictionary defines "Higher Powers" as spirits or beings (such as God) which have great power, strength, knowledge, etc. that can affect nature and the lives of people. In this chapter, we take a comical look at fictitious aficionados who attempt to negotiate life, death, wealth, or power with higher entities.

PROPHESY

A drag-racing driver John Force, 16-time NHRA champion with 151 career victories, put too much nitro methane in his slingshot dragster. The car ignited in a giant flame ball at the starting line. It blew him and his car to smithereens. His tombstone read: "HE IS MIST."

FAITH

A guy tried to drive across a flooded road and his car was swept into the rapidly rising river. A helpful trucker floated a life line to him, but he shouted: "I don't need it, I have faith in God, and He will save me!" So the trucker left, shaking his head. Soon the man's car filled up with water and he was standing on the roof of his car, the murky water swirling around him. Fire department rescue workers floated a rubber raft to him, but he shouted: "I don't need a raft, I have faith in God, and He will save me!" So he waved them off. Soon, a rescue helicopter flew overhead and dropped down a life jacket and rope ladder, and the pilot shouts: "Grab the ladder and climb up!" The stubborn guy shouted back: "Nope! I have faith in God, and He will save me." Soon the swirling floodwaters engulfed and drowned the man. Fortunately, he wound up at the Pearly Gates, face to face with God. "God", he said, "I was sure you would save me, but you let me down. Why, oh, why?" God replied sternly: "You jerk; I sent you a rope, a boat, and a helicopter!"

THE TEST

Herb, an old car guy, was quite religious. He was working late one night in his garage on his Corvette. God appeared to him: "If you had a million dollar beach house, would you give it to me?" "For sure," said Herb. "And if you had a collection of beautiful classic cars, would you give them all to me?" "Of course," said Herb. And then God said: "How about a Corvette?" And Herb replied: "That's not fair, God. You *know* I have a Corvette."

LET US PRAY

A Mom was driving her 5-year-old son to McDonald's one day and they passed a car accident and a bunch of drivers slowing down and gawking. Whenever the Mom saw something like that, she would always say a prayer for those who might be hurt, so she said to her son, "We should pray." From the back seat, she heard his earnest request: "Please, God, don't let those cars block the entrance to McDonald's."

MOSES' CHOICE

"Moses," said God, in his foreboding voice. "Look several thousand years into the future with cars and trucks spewing choking oily exhaust fumes. I will let you lead my people out of the desert if you can take them to a place without this dirty oil." Moses agrees, and after 40 years of leading the people of Israel to wander the desert, he took them to the Promised Land. Yes, it was Israel, the only Middle-Eastern country without oil!

(BONUS – Moses supposes his toeses are roses. BUT Moses supposes erroneously. For nobody's toeses are all made of roses, as Moses supposes his toeses to be!)

HELP ON THE WAY

A trucker broke down on a rural road, and hood open, he scratched his head. A minister happened by in a Model A Ford, and suggested that the trucker pray for help. "Good idea," said the trucker, as he raised his eyes to heaven. "Oh Lord, help me, a poor truck driver and miserable sinner, get this old truck running so I can get home." Just then a bolt of lightning came from the sky, struck the truck's carburetor, and instantly the motor started and hummed nicely. The minister, astonished, exclaimed: "Holy Crap, I'll be damned!"

THE MINISTER AND THE SCOTCH

A minister ran a red traffic light and crashed into a man's car. Both of their cars are demolished but amazingly neither of them was hurt. After they crawled out of their cars, the minister said, "Wow, just look at our cars! They are wrecked, but at least we are not hurt. This is surely a message from God that we should be friends." The man replied, "I agree with you completely. This must be a sign from God!" The minister continued, "And look at this, here's another miracle. My car is completely demolished, but my 75-year-old bottle of scotch didn't break. Surely God meant for us to share this vintage delicacy and celebrate our good fortune." The minister opened the bottle, sniffed its vintage fragrance, and handed it to the man. The fellow guzzled half the bottle and then handed it back to the minister to drink the other half bottle. The minister took the bottle, immediately put the cap back on, and handed it back to the man. The man asks, "Aren't you having any?" The minister replies, "Nah. I think I'll just wait for the police."*(adapted from wwwforums.poz.com)*

PRIEST GOT HIM ANYWAY

This one truck driver, Charlie, would often amuse himself by running over lawyers. Whenever he saw a lawyer on the sidewalk he would swerve off the road to hit him. Charlie enjoyed the loud, satisfying "THUMP" as he did so, and then would swerve his truck back onto the road. One day, as he was driving, he saw a priest hitch-hiking. He thought he'd do a good turn so he pulled the truck over and said to the priest, "Where're you going, Father?" The priest answered, "I'm going to the church three miles down the road." "No problem, Father!" said the trucker, "I'll give you a lift. Climb in." So the priest climbed into the passenger seat and the truck driver continued down the road. Soon the truck driver saw a lawyer on the sidewalk and quickly swerved towards him. But he suddenly remembered there was a priest in the truck with him, so at the last minute he swerved away, his right front fender just missing the lawyer. Even though he was sure he'd missed the lawyer, he still heard a loud "THUD". Not knowing where the noise had come from, he turned to the priest and said, "I'm sorry Father. I almost hit that lawyer." The priest said: "I know. Luckily, I got him with the door."*(adapted from www.laffgaff.com)*

ANYTHING FOR A TROPHY

Two buddies, Paul and Bay City Bob, loved winning trophies at car shows, and they even agreed that the one who died first would try to come back as an angel and tell the other if there were car shows with trophies in the afterlife. One summer night, Paul passed away in his sleep. A few nights later, his buddy Bob awoke to the sound of Paul's angelic voice from beyond. "Paul is that you?" Bob asked. "Of course it is me," Paul replied. "This is unbelievable," Bob exclaimed. "So tell me, are there car shows in heaven?" Paul said: "Well, I have some good news and some bad news for you. Which do you want to hear first?" "Tell me the good news first," said Bob. "Well the good news is that, yes Bob, there are car shows in heaven." "Oh that is wonderful! So what could possibly be the bad news?" said Bob. Paul said: "You compete for your first trophy up there tomorrow night."

DON GARLITS GOLFING

Don Garlits, the famous drag racing champion driver of his noted "Swamp Rat" dragster cars, went golfing with his minister. "Dammit," Don exclaimed, as he hit a long drive into the rough. The minister was shocked, and reminded Don that a man of the cloth does not appreciate swearing. "Certainly," Don replied with embarrassment. Then Don missed a five foot putt: "Damn! Missed again!" Again, the minister chided Don, telling him that God would punish him for swearing. "So sorry," Don sheepishly said. And they played on… until… Don chipped a shot way over the green into the sand trap. "Damn, missed again!", Don shouted at the top of his lungs. Before the minister could speak, the sky turned jet black, the thunder rolled, the clouds parted, and a golden flash of hot lightning streaked down from the heavens, across the sky, down to the golf course, and struck. Struck…the minister…dead. Then a mighty voice from the sky exclaimed: "DAMN! MISSED AGAIN!"

TIME WARP

A car guy looks into the sky and asks "God, how much is a million years to you???"

God's voice booms down, "ONE SECOND!"

The guy asks "God, how much is a million dollars to you???"

God's voice answers powerfully, "ONE PENNY!"

The guy politely requests, "God, could I please have a completely restored 1955 Crown Victoria, black and yellow, with all the options???"

God replies "SURE, JUST A SECOND".

HENRY FORD AT THE PEARLY GATES

Henry Ford died rich and "wanted to take it with him." At the Pearly Gates, it was fortunate that St. Peter really liked the neat Fords which he had built, so St. Peter agreed that he could go back to earth and bring just one suitcase of stuff into heaven, whatever he wanted. Old Henry quickly went back to his bank and stuffed a big suitcase full of gold coins, so heavy he could barely lift it. He again appeared at the Pearly Gates, and immediately encountered St. Peter. Henry greedily opened the suitcase to show St. Peter thousands of shining $1,000 gold pieces. "Pavement?" St. Peter exclaimed. "Why in heaven's name would you bring pavement?"

TOBY, JIM, AND JOHNNY MEET ST. PETER

In the far distant future, Toby appeared at the Pearly Gates, and St. Peter said: "You have led an exemplary life, started a cool car club, ran an honest business, been a good husband, so you get to drive a 1956 Crown Vic Glasstop around in heaven. The next guy to appear was Jim from Virginia, and St. Peter said: "I'm going to let you in because you were a pretty fun guy. You built your own 1954 Ford museum, but I happen to like the old Hudsons more. Also, you were a Republican and I am a Democrat, so you only get to drive a Yugo in heaven. The third guy to appear was nicknamed Johnny. St. Peter said: "Johnny, you just barely made it in, so here. You told many tall tales, and rumor has it that you were a moonshine runner. But you did help your friends make those old Y-Blocks run fast. So...take these roller skates!!!"

EARNHARDT, JOHNSON AND TURNER MEET ST. PETER

Three famous race car drivers—Junior Johnson, Curtis Turner, and Dale Earnhardt, Sr. had a terrific NASCAR crash and all appeared together at the Pearly Gates. St.

Peter said to Dale Earnhardt: "Dale, you were a tough guy on the NASCAR track, but you started a charitable organization at Clemson University, so you get to ride around in heaven in a $500,000 AC Cobra. Here are the keys, Enjoy!" Next up was Junior Johnson: "Junior", said St. Peter, "you are both good and bad. You stretched the rules in NASCAR until they snapped and you spent a year in jail for having an illegal moonshine still. However, you always bring topnotch moonshine to a party, so you are going to make our get-togethers more fun. Here are the keys to a 1971 Mustang with a 429 Cobra Jet engine. Have fun!" Finally, Curtis Turner stepped to the fore. St. Peter said: "Curtis, you have a reputation, mostly all bad. A book about you says you are 'NASCAR's First Bad Boy.' An internet post on you is 'Wood, Whiskey, Women and Winning.' You drove so hard that your nickname is 'Pops' because you popped people from behind and spun them out." St. Peter continued: "I respect your driving style, so I will let you into heaven—just barely. Here is your key." Curtis says: "Thanks, but this is a weird looking key." St. Peter replies: "It's for your Vespa motor scooter."

JUST REWARD

Cranky old Charles Goodyear passed on and appeared at the gates of Hades, shouting: "I built millions of tires for cars for the American people, so I don't belong here!" Lucifer said: "But you were nasty, cruel, and mean. You worked your employees six days a week 12 hours a day for low pay, and they were miserable." Then Lucifer opened a red door and there was a lovely-looking lady, and Charles Goodyear was puzzled: "So why did you show me that gorgeous blonde?" Goodyear drooled with lust: "Is she my reward?" "No", St. Peter said, "This woman was worse than you and terribly evil, so you are her punishment."

GOODNESS OVERFLOWS

Minister Goodman and used car Salesman Slicker were in a head-on crash and appeared at the Pearly Gates at the same time. St. Peter said to the Minister Goodman: "Welcome to heaven, Reverend, here are your accommodations." His room was small and plain, just barely OK. Then St. Peter said to Salesman Slicker: "Welcome to heaven, Mr. Slicker, and you may have a grand suite with A-1 service." The Reverend challenged St. Peter: "I'm a humble man of the cloth. Yet the salesmen spent his life in pursuit of ill-gotten financial profit. It's just not fair!" St. Peter replied: "We have an oversupply of ministers here and are running out of room for them. But, used car salesmen rarely appear in heaven, and he's our first one this year!"

CAREFUL WHAT YOU WISH FOR

Two priests died at the same time and met Saint Peter at the Pearly Gates. St. Peter said, "I'd like to get you guys in now, but our computer is down. You'll have to go back to Earth for about a week, but you can't go back as priests. So what else would you like to be?" The first priest says, "I've always wanted to be an eagle, soaring above the Rocky Mountains." "So be it," says St. Peter, and off flies the first priest. The second priest mulls this over for a moment and asks, "Will any of this week 'count', St. Peter?" "No, I told you the computer's down. There's no way we can keep track of what you're doing." "In that case," says the second priest, "I've always wanted to be a big stud, never having had a woman. I want to stay hard as steel all week. And I want to be safe, if you know what I mean, so please provide rubber for protection, if you know what I mean." "So be it", says St. Peter, and the second priest lustfully disappears. A week goes by, the computer is fixed, and the Lord tells St. Peter to recall the two priests. The Lord asks: "Will you have any trouble locating them?" "The first one should be easy," says St. Peter. "He's somewhere over the Rockies, soaring with the eagles." "And the other priest?" asked the Lord. St. Peter replied: "He's a steel stud on a snow tire, somewhere in Northern Canada."

IT'S THE PRAYERS THAT COUNT

A minister dies and gets in line at the Pearly Gates. Just ahead of him is a hippie dressed in wild sunglasses, slicked back hair, t-shirt with cigarette pack rolled up in the sleeve, Harley jacket, and rattlesnake leather boots. Saint Peter says to the hippie: "Who are you, and why should I let you into the Kingdom of Heaven?" The hippie replies, "I'm Slick Sloan, taxi-driver, of New York City." Saint Peter consults his sacred list, smiles and says to the taxi-driver: "You may enter into the Kingdom to live on a cloud of gold." Then the minister is next in line. Without being asked, he proclaims, "I am Father Michael O'Connor, head pastor of Saint Mary's for the last forty-three years." Saint Peter consults his sacred list and says: "You may enter the kingdom and live on a plain white cloud." "Just a minute," the minister says. "Why do I get a plain white cloud while the hippie taxi driver gets a golden cloud?" Saint Peter says: "Up here we go by prayer results. While you preached, people slept. While he drove, people prayed."

LEE IACOCCA AT THE PEARLY GATES

Lee Iacocca dies and goes to the Pearly Gates. St. Peter tells Lee: "Well, you've been such a good guy, coined the phrase 'a '55 Ford for $55 a month' and more. You saved Chrysler from going under. As a reward you can hang out with anybody of your choice in Heaven." So Lee Iacocca thinks about it and says: "I would like to talk with God himself". So St. Peter takes him directly to God and Lee Iacocca says: "God, I don't want to sound rude, but you have some engineering problems in Your Invention, the Woman. First, her front end is a distraction. Second, it is often loud and noisy. Third, the rear end shakes too much and causes men nothing but trouble." God is taken back, but being perfect in all ways, he thinks fast. God then turns to Lee Iacocca and says; "It may be that *my invention* is a bit loud, distracting, and troubling to men, but men still enjoy riding my creations more than yours."

MEDDLING PREACHER

Two car guys went to church together, and the preacher repeatedly denounced gambling, smoking, drinking, and pot smoking—to which the guys responded: "AAAA-MEN!" Then the preacher talked about the problems caused by gasoline burning engines causing air pollution and global warming. Then one car guy said to the other: "Wouldn't you know it? He stopped preaching and now he's meddling!"

VOCABULARY

Did you hear about the minister who bought a broken down old Chevy but then his bishop informed him that he was not allowed to use his total vocabulary when driving it?

A BIG THANK YOU

A teenager who had just received her learner's permit offered to drive her parents to church. After a hair-raising ride, they finally reached their destination. The mother got out of the car and said, "Thank you!" "Any time," her daughter replied. As the mother slammed the door, she said, "I wasn't talking to you. I was talking to God."

LIKE CHANGING PEE INTO GAS?

A couple of nuns who worked as nurses had driven an old 1987 Jeep Wrangler out to the countryside to treat patients. On the way back home, they ran out of gas. They were standing beside their Jeep on the shoulder when a truck approached. Seeing the nuns there, the driver stopped to help. The nuns said their gas tank was empty. The trucker said he had no gas can, but the nuns thought fast and came up with a bedpan. So the trucker put some truck gas into the bedpan and the nuns were pouring it into their Jeep when a cop drove up. With a smile, he said: "Bless you Sisters, if you think your faith is strong enough to turn pee into gas."

TRUST IN GOD

You can tell that Americans trust in God by the way they drive their old Jeeps.

CAR GUY PRAYER

"Lord, I ask nothing for myself, but will you please send dear wife a 1955 red and white Thunderbird with stick shift and overdrive?"

LOST IN A TORNADO

Arnie Sr., a wealthy gent, was driving his restored 1958 Plymouth Fury, one of the 17 Fury's not crushed in a famous movie, "Christine". Suddenly, a huge storm came and a tornado scooped him and his car up into the violent sky. He held tight to the steering wheel and he screamed a prayer to God: "Oy vey, please save me and my rare and beautiful car, Oh God." Within minutes, the weather calmed, and he and his car were settled gently back on the highway, no harm done. Arnie Sr. breathed a prayer of thanks, but added: "God, do not think me ungrateful, but...I also had a hat."

TOO MANY BLESSINGS

A Peace Corps minister in South America was furiously driving his open Jeep down a dirty, rutted road, hurrying to get to a remote village on time. Suddenly he hit a huge bump and was thrown out of the Jeep, which luckily slowed to a stop in the mud. Lying in the mud, with sprained ankles, his body wracked with pain, the minister called out: "All you angels in heaven, help me get up on the seat in my Jeep!" With extraordinary strength and pain, he leaped toward the Jeep—and fell over the tops of the seats out to the other side of the Jeep into the mud. From the mud hole, he again called out, "All right, just *half* of you angels this time!"

THE GOOD THIEF

A thief was feeling guilty and wanted to confess. Fortunately, he was a Catholic so he went to Father Peter in the confessional to receive the sacrament of penance: "Bless me Father, for I have sinned, my last confession was a year ago." The Priest said: "Tell me, my son, what sin have you committed?" The thief confessed: "I broke a commandment, Father. I stole four classy TBird spinner hubcaps and sold them for $150. Can I give you the $150, Father?" The Priest replied: "No, I don't want the money; you must offer the money to your victim." The thief replied: "I did offer the money to my victim, Father, and he said he did not want it." Father said: "In that case, you may keep the money. Say five Our Fathers and five Hail Mary's and an Act of Contrition. Go and sin no more." After hearing confessions that day, Father Peter returned to the rectory where he lived. He noticed his car was missing four spinner hubcaps!

TO DUST YE SHALL RETURN

After an uncle's funeral service, little Johnny asked his father, a preacher, and owner of a '55 Cadillac: "What did the minister mean about ashes to ashes and dust unto dust?" The minister promptly took his Bible and looked up Genesis 3:19 and read: "By the sweat of your face you shall eat bread, 'til you return to the ground, for out of it you were taken; for you are dust and to dust you shall return." Johnny said: "Wow, dad, you don't ever clean your car, so I guess there is either someone coming or someone going."

FOR THE SICK

On this special Sunday, Dad Otto pulled his 1953 Buick out of the garage for St. Christopher's Church. Meanwhile, Father Rupert had just finished building a new donation box for the church door entrance. His sign on it said "FOR THE SICK". During the church service, the little girl, Jeannie, started feeling ill, and said: "Daddy, can we leave now, I have a sick stomach". Daddy Otto said, no, not now. Little Jeannie said: "But I have to throw up!!" Dad said: "Then go out the door and around to the back of the church by the trees and throw up behind a bush." She said OK, but after about 60 seconds little Jeannie returned to her seat. "Did you throw up?", Dad Otto asked. "Yes," she said. "But how could you have gone all the way outside the church and found a bush and returned so quickly?" "I didn't have to go way behind the church, Daddy. They have a box next to the front door that says, 'FOR THE SICK.'"

PROMISE BIG

The old Priest at a Catholic Church, Father Rupert, loved old cars and decided to have a car show to raise money for the parish building fund. The flyer promised all Catholics "Days off from Purgatory" for bringing classic cars. The promised grand prize was a certificate which said: "Guaranteed Entrance to Heaven".

PREACHER SAW THE LIGHT

Overheard from a tent preacher in the Deep South in a tent revival: "When I was young, I used to pray that God would give me a 1963 XL500 Galaxie convertible. Now I realize that it doesn't work that way. So I stole the convertible, and then asked God for forgiveness."

PETTY, FOYT, AND BUSCH BEAT SATAN

Due to a terrible crash and a worse mistake, three fine race car drivers wound up facing Satan at the Gates of Hell—Richard Petty, A.J. Foyt, and Kyle Busch. Realizing where they were, they each mounted a vigorous defense of the good they had done in life. "Satan," said Kyle Busch, "I was generous with the money I won in racing and I gave my time and money to children's hospitals." Satan thought, you are an OK guy, and you do not deserve hellfire. Then came Richard Petty, who said: "Satan, I was nicknamed 'The King' for winning the Daytona 500 and the national championship each seven times during 1964-1981. I do not accept alcohol sponsorships, and I was awarded the Medal of Freedom by President George Bush in 1992, and I'm the first motor sports driver ever to receive this award. This is a mistake that I am at Satan's gates." Satan nodded in agreement. Then stood A.J. Foyt, who stated that he was the only driver to win the Indy 500, the Daytona 500, the 24 hours of Daytona, and the 24 Hours of LeMans. Foyt then said: "Also, I believe in strong American families, and I am my brother's keeper, so I adopted a boy and I am the godfather of driver John Adretti." Satan thought: "This guy is a saint in my book—but—what to do? What to do? What to do?" As evil as Satan was, he considered himself a hell-of-a-guy, but he hated to lose a soul. So he issued an impossible challenge to Petty, Foyt, and Busch: "You guys are car nuts, so if each of you can come up with a car named after me, the Great Satan, or my home Hades, I will let you go see St. Peter. Richard Petty, you are first." Petty thought and thought and then it came to him. "The Crosley Hotshot," he exclaimed. "It was American's first sports car, made from 1948-1952, only 26 HP, and did 71 MPH. It weighed 1,000 lbs. and cost $1,000." Satan said: "Good enough, Mr. Petty, you are free to see St. Peter." Then Satan turned his eyes to A. J. Foyt, and waited. Foyt exclaimed: "The Lamborghini Diablo! It was the first Lambo capable of 200 MPH, was made from 1990-2001, and only 2,484 were ever produced." Satan was stunned, and said: "OK, Foyt, go see Peter at the Pearly Gates." But Satan did not really want to lose all three of these great prizes, so he issued this challenge to Kyle Busch: "Mr. Busch, you must top the responses of your two colleagues if you want to declare victory and get out of Dodge, so to speak." Kyle was stumped, but Satan's words washed over him—"Dodge!" He shouted. "Dodge, Dodge, and Dodge. From 1970-1972 there was the Dodge Demon and even the advertising brochure described it as tough as a Little Devil! Then in 2018 came the Dodge Challenger SRT Demon, the world's first production car to lift the front wheels at launch. And then there's the Dodge Challenger SRT Hellcat with 707 HP..." Exasperated, Satan stopped him: "OK, OK, OK...you got me. NOW GET THE HELL OUT OF HERE!"

EDSEL FORD AT THE GATES OF HELL

Edsel Ford was not as successful as his father and when he died, he appeared at the Gates of Hell, and the Devil was there to admit him. Edsel asked if there were highways in hell. "Oh, yes,", replied the Devil, "four-lane highways and beautiful country roads everywhere." Edsel smiled. "And what about 104 octane gasoline?", Edsel asked. "You bet", said the Devil, "Shell, Texaco, Sunoco, all brands!" Then Edsel asked, "And cars", Edsel asked, "What brands of cars?" The Devil frowned sadly, "NO CARS, no cars at all...that's the hell of it".

SHELBY REHN

PALMIST

A fellow went to Madam Mystere fortune teller to read the future from the creases in his palm. He wanted to know the future. She said: "I foresee that the 454 engine in your 1972 Monte Carlo is going to fail catastrophically and an engine fire will burn your car up because you did not have a fire extinguisher with you." He said: "That's amazing. But all that happened two months ago." She said: "Ah, but you haven't washed your hands for two months!"

WISH FOR THE GENIE

Hoppy was walking along the beach and accidentally kicked a brass lamp, and a genie popped out. The genie offered him one wish. Hoppy had always wanted a glitzy Ford, but didn't have the money. So he said: "Genie, build me a customized 1956 Glasstop Crown Victoria. I want pink and white interior and exterior, a hopped up 312 with 3-2 carbs, glass packs, cruiser skirts, continental kit, flamethrowers, and hydraulics so I can lower it into the weeds." The genie said, "Your request has enormous challenges! The parts will take a while to get. The expertise to build such a car—very few genies know this kind of work. And it's so materialistic! Why not take a little more time and think of something which will contribute to your personal growth? More knowledge to share with mankind?" Hoppy thought about his wife Tonda...hmmm. Finally he said, "Genie, I wish that I could understand women, I want to know how they feel inside, what they are thinking when I get the silent treatment, why they cry for no reason, why they are angry but they say 'nothing's wrong,' and the secret to making my woman truly happy." The genie paused and then replied..."You want wide whites on that Crown?"

SAINT PETER WRITES A LETTER

Robin and Phil, avid kayakers, accidentally paddled their canoes over Niagara Falls, and before they dashed to the rocks below, they were swiftly transported by angels to St. Peter. "Wow", they said, "We're sure glad we were good. Now can we kayak in heaven?" St. Peter said: "Yes. We have pleasant streams everywhere, with all kinds of lovely trees, and you will enjoy it greatly." St. Peter also said: "You two are unique in that you both have absolutely perfect driving records. No road rage, no speeding tickets, no parking infractions, no DWI's—nothing!" St. Peter continued: "In fact, more living humans should be like you both, and do exemplary driving as a way to get into heaven. So right now, I am going to write every human who drives safely a letter congratulating them on their perfect driving." *(And do you know what that letter said??? You don't? Well, darn it, I didn't get one either.)*

FOUR RIDDLES: CARS IN THE BIBLE

1) Q: How do we know that cars are in the New Testament?

A: Because Jesus was a car painter!

2) Q: What kind of loud English car is in the Bible?

A: David's Triumph was heard throughout the land.

3) Q: What kind of Japanese car is in the Bible?

A: Honda...because the apostles were all in one Accord.

4) Q: What kind of Mopar car is in the Bible?

A: Jehovah drove Adam and Eve out of the Garden in a Fury.

CHAPTER TEN

AUTO AFICIONADOS DEAL WITH EARTHLY AUTHORITIES (POLICE, JUDGES, FIREMEN, ETC.)

In a more "down to earth" realm, aficionados must risk daily encounters with police, judges, clerks at the motor vehicle administration, firemen, drunks, thieves, and other close encounters of the second kind while on the highway. In this book, all encounters will make you chuckle.

HARD JUDGE

Recently, in a Traffic Court, Bernie who received an expensive parking ticket for his 1969 Chevelle, testified that a uniformed policeman had given his "OK" to park there since it was for a classic car show to benefit needy children. Judge Ironside asked the man if he would recognize the officer if he ever saw him again, and the man replied that he would. The Judge then said, "Good. When you see the officer again, tell him he owes you 57 dollars. Next…"

50 DOLLARS

Judge Ironside: "I'm going to give you ten days or 50 dollars for drinking and driving."

Defendant: "Great! I'll take the 50 dollars!"

JUST ANOTHER DRUNK

Judge Ironside: "The policeman brought you here for drinking."

Drunk: "Great! Let's get started!"

GOOD EXCUSE #1

Judge Ironside: "Sir you were arrested for driving 90 miles an hour though town with your headlights off. Why?"

Prisoner: "I had to, Judge, the car was stolen."

GOOD EXCUSE #2

Judge Ironside: "Madam, you were arrested for driving 85 miles an hour in a rainstorm this afternoon. Why?"

Prisoner: "Judge, my brakes weren't working at all, and I was hurrying to get home before I had an accident."

DUMB CAR THIEVES

A witness is testifying before the court, and the prosecuting attorney is asking him questions:

The Prosecutor: "You witnessed the car theft, sir?"

The Eyewitness: "Yes"

The Prosecutor: "What was stolen?"

The Eyewitness: "A 1971 baby blue Monte Carlo with 454 engine."

The Prosecutor: "Did you see the thieves?"

The Eyewitness: "Yes."

The Prosecutor: "Could you identify them?"

The Eyewitness: "Yes"

The Prosecutor, in a bold voice: "ARE THE TWO MEN WHO STOLE THE CAR PRESENT IN THIS COURTROOM???"

(At this point, the two defendants quickly raised their hands.)

THE JAILBIRD'S LESSON

A long-haired teenage kid, James, fell in love with his lovely English teacher. So he stole a car so he could propose to her and they could elope. But the cops quickly caught him and put him in jail for a one-year sentence. James propositioned her with marriage after he got out, but she refused. Alas, as his lovely teacher had taught him, he found that you can't end a sentence with a proposition.

DESCRIPTION NEEDED

Big Mike called his car-rental company and said his hybrid electric rental car needed to be towed. Big Mike named Highway 50 and Exit 37 where he was stranded -- but he could no longer discern the color of the car he was driving. The Hertz representative asked for a more detailed description: "Is it a two-door or a four-door?" After a pause, Mike replied: "It's the one on fire."

DREW AT THE MVA

When Andrew (nicknamed "Drew") went to get his driver's license renewed, the Glen Burnie motor-vehicle department had a line out the door. The line inched along for three hours until Drew finished the paperwork and got to the photographer. She snapped his photo. Drew looked at it and said it was his worst photo ever: "I look so grouchy," he said apologetically. The clerk looked at his picture: "It's okay," she reassured Drew. "That's how unhappy you will appear when the police 'light you up' when you get caught speeding."

MD DRIVER'S LICENSE
D-222-567-890
LAST NAME: GRUMP
FIRST NAME: DREW
DOB: 05/22/1946
113 GROUCHINGTON LN
GRUMPVILLE MD 22345

SHELBY REHN

SHELBY SPEEDING DOWN THE HIGHWAY

Shelby was a young lady driving on the dotted line in the center of the road at 100 mph. A police officer red-lighted her and pulled her over to the side of the road. When Shelby had stopped, the officer politely asked, "License and Registration please." "It's okay, Officer, I have a special license that allows me to drive in the middle of the road," she said smiling. "That's impossible!", the officer replied, "I've never heard of such a license." Shelby reached into her purse and handed him her license. Astonished, the officer said, "Just as I suspected. This is an ordinary license. I see nothing here that would allow you special consideration." Shelby pointed to the bottom of the license: "See? It says so right here, 'Tear along the dotted line'."

COMMANDER COMMANDEERED

On base, my Commanding Officer told me to take his Jeep Commander and get an oil change. As I near the Jiffy Lube, a lady is walking by the side of the road. Suddenly, a deer pulls a knife and pushes it into her stomach and she backs up towards my Jeep. The deer forces the lady to get in the driver's seat and push me to the side, and then she just starts driving. She's excited and almost immediately she hits a tree. The deer is still in the passenger seat with a knife pushed up to her stomach. The police ask for an explanation, and all I can tell him is that a common deer commanded her to commandeer my commander's Commander.

STOP HIM!

At Driver's School in St. Michael's, Maryland, the Police Instructor stated: "Did you know that, in Maryland, there is a fender-bender every 30 seconds." Shawn, a guy sitting in the back, was astounded by that worrisome statistic, and shouted: "We've got to find that guy and stop him!"

MAKES YOUR HEART RACE

Sometimes someone unexpected comes into your life out of nowhere, makes your heart race, and changes you for years. Those sometimes are called "cops"!

DISTRACTIONS

Debbie was driving her daughter Julia's blue-VW Bug and had a flat tire on I-66 in Virginia. So she pulled over to the side of her road and popped her hood. She took out two full-sized cardboard men, and propped them up at the rear of her car, to face oncoming traffic. They had open trench coats that exposed their nude bodies which were anatomically correct. Cars slowed down, tooted their horns, and gave thumbs up. Soon a state trooper pulled up and asked: "What's going on?" "I have a flat tire," Debbie said sheepishly. "Well, what the heck are those obscene cardboard men doing here by your car?" Debbie smiled broadly and said: "I'll give you a hint. Those are my emergency flashers!"

ROOKIE TRAVIS

A rookie police officer named Travis was assigned to a rough part of town. The chief's call came over Travis' radio telling him to disperse some people who were loitering on a corner. The rookie drove to a near corner and saw a small crowd standing there. Travis rolled down his window, grabbed his megaphone, and shouted: "Move along and get off the corner. No loitering!" No one moved, so he barked louder: "Move along! Now!" Intimidated, the people started to shuffle away, with resentful and confused looks on their faces. Proud of his first official act, rookie Travis then saw the sign: "BUS STOP."

DESIGNATED DRIVER FUN

Did your inebriated friends designate you to be designated driver? Have some fun. Drop them off at an Alcoholics Anonymous meeting.

BOTH CHARGED

Did you hear about the cop who caught two teens stealing two batteries? He charged them both.

FIFTH ON FOURTH

With the Fourth of July approaching, the police developed a slogan and put up posters around town discouraging drinking over the holiday weekend. The slogan was: "He who comes forth with a fifth on the Fourth may not come forth on the Fifth."

THE COLLECTION OFFICER

OFFICER: Here is your speeding ticket.

DRIVER: What am I supposed to do with it?

OFFICER: Save it. When you collect six of them, you get a bicycle.

BILLY JOEL'S FAVORITE JOKE

Gangsters in a big black Caddy machine-gunned a police car. It was a case of Cadillac-ack-ack-ack-ack-ack-ack.

STOLEN CAR

A drunk called 911 and told the police that thieves had been in his car. "They've stolen my spare tire, my jack, and a toolbox," he complained. However, before the cops could arrive, he called them back. In the same slurred voice, he told them: "Never mind. I got in the trunk by mistake."

TO AMUSE YOURSELF

Sit in a plain car wearing sunglasses. Park on a busy street. Point a hair dryer at each passing car (except police cars).

WATER TO WINE?

A highway patrol officer was driving behind a man who was swerving all over the road. The officer stopped the man and asked, "Sir, have you been drinking?" The man said, "Shurr, I'm a priest. I drink wine every time I say Mass." The officer asked, "What is in that wine bottle beside you?" The priest said, "Water, of cour-she!" The officer opened the bottle, took a sniff, and said, "Reverend, there is wine in this bottle!" The priest then replied, "Praishe the Lord, he has done it again!"

CLOSER

A young lady is taking the road test for her driver's license for the third time. She really wanted to pass this time. She finally handled the open road test OK, but when she parallel-parked, she was almost three feet from the curb. The sympathetic police examiner said politely: "Could you get a little closer please?" She puts her car in park, unsnapped the seat belt, and slid across the seat next to him. Then she said coyly: "Now what?"

PATRIOTISM

It's funny how the patriotic colors of red, white, and blue make us proud to stand tall. However, when they are revolving lights in your rear-view mirror, we tend to shrink down in the seat.

TIPS

Police officer Travis had a new perfect hiding place for watching for speeders. But soon, everyone he clocked was well under the speed limit. After some investigative work, the officer found the cause. A 12-year-old boy was standing on the curb with a sign that said: "RADAR TRAP AHEAD." His friend was 100 yards further down the road with a bucket at his feet which said "TIPS".

BAD SPELLER?

County traffic policeman Travis stopped a woman for exceeding the posted speed limit. He asked the driver her name…she said, "I'm Mrs. Ladislav Abdulkhashim Zybkcicraznovskays from the Republic of Uzbekistan visiting my daughter in college in America." The cop put away his summons book and pen, and said, "Welll… OK…but don't let me catch you speeding again." *(adapted from www.webby.com).*

TOO MANY TICKETS

Cindy went to Love Point Deli the other day, in her MG, and she was only in there for about five minutes. When she came out there was a traffic cop writing a parking ticket for a light blue Mercury. She was slightly outspoken, so she went up to him and said, "Come on copper, have a heart!" He ignored her and continued writing the ticket. So she called him a "pencil-necked wimp." He glared at her and wrote a second ticket for a bald tire! So she called him a "bird brain." He started writing a third ticket! This went on for another 15 minutes. The more she insulted him, the more tickets he wrote. She didn't care! Her MG was parked around the corner. A lady named Sandy wound up getting all the tickets.

I KNOW DA' GUY

An immigrant goes to the DMV to apply for a driver's license. He has to take an eyesight test. The police examiner shows him a card with the letters C Z J W I X N O S T A C Z. "Can you read this?" the examiner asks. In a heavy accent the man replied: "Read dis? I tink I know da' guy."

DUELING PHOTOS

A motorist was mailed pictures of his car speeding through an automated radar post in Stevensville, MD. A $40 speeding ticket was included. Being cute, he sent the police department a picture of two $20 bills. The police responded with another mailed photo of handcuffs.

(adapted from www.forums.gentoo.com)

SOOOO OBEDIENT

Officer Travis was parked behind a billboard sign and saw a blonde woman puttering along at 18 MPH. So, he turns his red and blue lights on and pulls the car over. Inside are three ladies, one in the front, but the two in the back looked wide-eyed and terrified. The driver, Maureen, a blonde lady, obviously confused, said, "Officer, I don't understand, I wasn't doing over the speed limit. What seems to be the problem?" "Ma'am," Officer Travis said: "You know that driving slower than the speed limit can also be dangerous." Maureen replied: "Slower than the speed limit? No sir! I was doing exactly 18 miles an hour". The officer, smirking, explains that 18 was the route number, Route 18, not the speed limit. A bit embarrassed, Maureen grinned, thanking the officer for pointing out her error. Then the officer said: "Before I go ma'am, I have to ask, are the two ladies in the back OK?" He saw Wende and Diana in the back and they seemed badly shaken. They hadn't uttered a word all this time. Maureen replied: "Oh! They'll be alright in a minute, officer; we just got off Route 95."

MAKE UP YOUR MIND

Officer Travis stops a guy named Rich for speeding in his Triumph and asks him to see his license and registration. Rich replied in a huff: "Shucks, Officer Travis, I wish you cops would get your procedures ironed out. Just yesterday you took my license away and then today you want me to show it to you!"

TRUE POLICE STORY

Paul carried the Grand Marshal in the Island Day parade in his red '55 Ford Sunliner. He was lined up just behind the color guard and the Deputy Chief of Police. He confused 1st gear and reverse gear and bumped the Deputy's police car in front of him. He hit the cop's trailer ball with his bumper's license plate, so no real damage. But word got out and around with every cop around and they all snickered at him. It was a street fair; many cops had Main Street blocked off. As Paul was leaving at the end of the afternoon, he said goodbye to the Chief of Police Gary and said: "I apologize for hitting your Deputy in the ball." The Police Chief Gary replied with a snicker, "He probably deserved it."

TOO DRUNK

Cop: "Please step out of the car."

Drunk: "I'm too drunk. You get in."

SMART ALEC RYAN

Officer Barrett had gotten a radio report of a speeding Jeep and was ordered to catch him before he causes an accident. Eventually, along came a speeding Jeep and the Officer red-lighted him. To the Officer's surprise, it was his son, Ryan, who was embarrassed to see his Dad. Cynically, the Officer said: "Nice to see you son." Ryan thought fast and said: "Well, Dad, I got here as fast as I could."

REPEAT OFFENDER

Anthony, nicknamed "Ant", was driving down the road. He passed a traffic camera and saw it flash. Ant had never been caught on candid police camera before, so he slowed his car and ran the same route. Again, it flashed. So he slowed his car to a crawl and drove past the camera again. AGAIN, he saw the camera flash. Ant guessed that it must have a defect, and home he went. Weeks later Ant received three traffic fines in the mail. All three for the same infraction—"not wearing a seatbelt."

ILLEGAL TURN

Jason, in a hurry, was taking his 8-year-old son Kevin to school, made a turn at a red light where it was prohibited. "Uh-oh, I just made an illegal turn," the man said. "Aw, Dad, it's okay," son Kevin said. "The police car right behind us did the same thing."

(adapted from www.sparkpeople.com)

NO MONEY FOR GAS TO MAKE THE VAN GO

Susan and Peter, world travelers, went to Paris to steal precious paintings from the Louvre art museum. After plotting the crime, renting a van, breaking into the museum, avoiding security, sneaking out, and escaping with the goods, they were spotted. In their haste, they had to leave several valuable paintings behind. They were captured by the cops only two blocks away when their van ran out of gas!

When asked how they could make such a stupid error, Peter replied: "We had no Monet to buy Degas to make the Van Gogh!"

A BRIDGE TOO LOW

Charlie the truck driver was driving along on the freeway. He missed seeing a sign that read, "LOW BRIDGE AHEAD." Before he knew it, the bridge was right ahead of him and he got wedged under it. Cars were backed up for miles. Finally a police car arrived. The cop got out of his car and walked around to the truck driver, put his hands on his hips and said, "Got stuck, huh?" Charlie the truck driver said, "No, smarty, I was delivering this bridge and ran out of gas."

MISSED THE TREES?

Robb was driving home in his macho Ford truck, drunk as a skunk. He usually did not drink that much, but he was celebrating a pickle ball victory. Suddenly he swerved to avoid a tree, than another, then another. A cop pulled him over, so he told the cop about all the trees in the road. The cop said, "That's your air freshener swinging from your rear-view mirror."

A FALLING OUT

Farmer John's truck was weaving wildly all over the road and a cop was following him for several miles and he finally sees the cop's gumball lights and stops. He fesses up…"Ya' got me." The cop says "Did you know your wife fell out two miles ago?" Farmer John, drunk, says "Thank God, I stopped hearing screaming and I thought I was going deaf."

PULL OVER

"Hey you!", shouted the motorcycle cop to Terry, speeding female driver, "Pull over!" Terry complied with the officer's request. The next day the judge fined her $75. Terry returned home from court with great anxiety lest her husband, Jim, who always examined her checkbook, should learn of the incident. The inspiration struck and Terry marked the check stub, "One pullover - $75."

NEW SOBRIETY TEST?

A juggler, driving to his next performance, is stopped by Officer Barrett. "What are those machetes doing in your car?" asks the cop. "I juggle them in my act." "Oh, yeah?" says the doubtful cop. "Let's see you do it." The juggler gets out and starts tossing and catching the knives. Another man driving by slows down to watch. "Wow," says the passer-by, "I'm glad I quit drinking. Look at the test they're giving now!"

MISSING BODY

Tyler the cop stopped a lady named Carol for speeding. He asked to see her license and registration. She said: "Sorry, it's not here, I stole this car. Also, I chopped up the owner and stuffed his body in the trunk." Her friend, Art, sitting next to her, gulped in dismay. Startled, Tyler the cop called for backup and in five minutes Carol and Art were surrounded by cop cars. The excited Chief Gary said to Carol: "My officer Tyler here says you stole the car and chopped up the owner's body and put the pieces in the trunk." "Nonsense", says Carol: "See, here is my license, here is my lawful registration". Then she popped the trunk and it was empty. Then she said to Chief Gary: "I bet that lying cop Tyler also told you I was speeding."

VIRGINIA COP NABS DEBBIE

Debbie was speeding at well over 80 miles an hour when she passed a Virginia State Trooper. He pulled her over and asked to see her license. After looking it over, he said, "It says right here on your license that you oughta should be wearing glasses." "I have contacts," Debbie retorted. "Look lady, I don't care who you know," snapped the officer. "You're getting a ticket."

ID

A Virginia State Trooper pulls Hoppy over on for speeding. He says to the driver, "Got any ID?" Hoppy says, "Bout what?"

SCARF!

Tyler, a highway patrolman in Maryland, pulled alongside a car weaving lanes on the freeway. He was astounded to see that the lady behind the wheel was knitting! Realizing that she was oblivious to his flashing lights and siren, Trooper

Tyler cranked down his window, turned on his bullhorn and yelled, "PULL OVER!" "NO!" the lady yelled back, "IT'S A SCARF!"

A SENSITIVE OFFICER

Tyler the police officer called the station on his radio. "I have an interesting case here. A guy was waxing his Boss 429 Mustang convertible and shot his wife because she gave him a dirty towel and it scratched the paint a bit." The radio cop said: "Have you arrested the man?" Tyler the cop said: "Not yet. He hasn't finished waxing the car yet."

CARDIAC ARREST?

A car thief was stealing Cadillac car parts from the hospital emergency parking lot. He got caught by cops. He was startled and his heart suddenly stopped. It was a case of Cadillac arrest.

TREASURED ONE PATTY MISSING

Larry went to the police station to report Patty, his missing wife:

Larry: "I've lost my wife, she went shopping yesterday and has still not come home."

Sergeant: "What is her height?"

Larry: "Oh, 5 something. . ."

Sergeant: "Build?"

Larry: "Not too slim, just like I like her."

Sergeant: "Color of eyes?"

Larry: "Never noticed."

Sergeant: "Color of hair?"

Larry: "Changes according to season."

Sergeant: "What was she wearing?"

Larry: "Dress/suit/blue jeans -- I don't remember exactly."

Sergeant: "Did she go in a car?'

Larry: "Yes."

Sergeant: "What kind of car was it?"

Larry: "1956 Ford Sunliner, Fiesta Red with red and white interior, 292 Y-Block, continental kit, glass packs, and has a very thin scratch on the front left door. (At this point the husband started crying.)

Sergeant: "Don't worry sir, we'll find your car."

(adapted from www.stevericherbooks.com)

SEVEN THINGS *NOT* TO SAY TO A POLICE OFFICER

1. "I can't reach my license unless you hold my beer."

2. "Sorry, officer, I didn't realize my radar detector wasn't plugged in."

3. "Aren't you the guy from the Village People?"

4. "Hey, you must've been doing about 125 mph to keep up with me. Good job!"

5. "Are you Andy or Barney?"

6. "Gee, I thought you had to be in relatively good physical condition to be a police officer."

7. "You're not gonna check the trunk, are you?"

(adapted from www.computerjy.com)

SHELBYREHN

SIX POLICE BACKATCHA'S

1. "So you don't know how fast you were going. I guess that means I can write anything I want on the ticket, huh?"

2. "Warning? You want a warning? O.K., I'm warning you to not speed again or I'll give you another ticket."

3. "You didn't think we give pretty women tickets? You're right, we don't. Sign here."

4. "Yes, we do have a quota. Two more tickets and my wife gets a toaster oven."

5. "No sir, we don't have quotas anymore. We used to have quotas but now we're allowed to write as many tickets as we want."

6. "Just how big were those two beers?"

COPS ARE FUNNY SIX TIMES OVER

1. "You know, stop lights don't come any redder than the one you just went through."

2. "Yes, sir, you can talk to the shift supervisor, but I don't think it will help. Oh, did I mention that I'm the shift supervisor?"

3. "The answer to this last question will determine whether you are drunk or not. Answer quick: Was Mickey Mouse a cat or a dog?"

4. "Fair? You want me to be fair? Listen, fair is a place where you go to ride on rides, eat cotton candy and corn dogs, and step in elephant poop."

5. "In God we trust; all others we run through the National Crime Information Center".

6. "I'm glad to hear that the Chief of Police is a personal friend of yours. So you know someone who can post your bail."

(adapted from www.dogbrothers.com)

FROM FOUR POLICE RECORDINGS OF ARRESTS

1. "Relax, the handcuffs are tight because they're new...they'll stretch out after you wear them a while."

2. "If you take your hands off the car, I'll make your birth certificate a worthless document."

3. "If you run...you'll only go to jail tired."

4. "Can you run faster than 1,200 feet per second? In case you didn't know, that is the average speed of a 9mm bullet fired from my gun."

(adapted from www.greekchat.com)

WESTERN AUTO CHATTER

Linda: "My favorite uncle built a radical custom car. He took the 429 Cobra Jet engine from a Ford, the C-6 transmission from a Mercury, the tires from a Cadillac Eldorado, the exhaust system from a RAM truck, the computer from a Lincoln Escalade, and the dash gauges from a Viper."

Doby: "Wow. What did he wind up with in the end?"

Linda: "Ten years for theft."

ONE-WAY RITA

Rita, an artist with a British accent who hated to drive, was navigating a narrow road when she was red-lighted by a cop. At her rolled-down window, he said: "Hey lady, don't you know that this is a one-way street?" Rita responded in her charming, polite, and correct British accent: "But officer, I'm only *going* one way!"

FAVORITE COLOR

In a small town, a driver flooded his carburetor and stalled out at a traffic light. A cop walked up to the driver's window, and tapped the driver's window as the light went from green to yellow to red, then green again. The cop said: "What's the matter? Haven't we got your favorite color?"

(adapted from www.issuu.com)

IN DISGUISE

A lady at the airport saw a police officer all dressed up as an airplane pilot. She concluded that he must be a plane clothes cop. *(Groan)*.

MIMI, OVER THE LIMIT

Mimi, an esthetician (beautician for the face), was in a hurry and driving 70 mph in a '55 mph zone. Tyler the cop "lit her up," and said: "Sorry ma'am, I have to ticket anyone over 55." Mimi protested: "Officer, that's age discrimination, and besides, while I am age 59, I am often told I *look* 39." As Mimi smiled sweetly, flirting, the cop explained: "I meant...over the speed limit."

JIM'S FIRE

A Virginia good ol' boy named Jimmy went to his private car museum in Colonial Beach and found his museum on fire. He rushed next door, phoned the fire department and shouted, "Hurry over here. My museum full of 1954 Fords is on fire!" "OK," replied the fireman, "How do we get there?" "Shucks," says Jimmy, "Don't y'all still have them big red trucks?"

CAT FIGHT ENDED

Four women working for the same auto dealership in the parts department of Koon's in Annapolis wanted the same premium parking space and it came to blows--a real cat fight. The dispute was of such magnitude that it resulted in their being hauled into court. When the case was called, they all made a concerted rush for the bench. Upon reaching it, all broke into bitter complaints at the same moment. Judge Ironside sat momentarily stunned as charges and counter-charges filled the air. Suddenly he rapped his hammer for order. When quiet had been restored, the patient magistrate said gently, "Now, I'll hear the oldest woman first." All was quiet. Case closed.

OFFICER MURPHY BIAS?

A Catholic priest, Father McDuffy, was mentally planning his next sermon while driving his van. Not paying attention, he rear-ended the Honda in front of him. Hard. His radiator hissed steam. He crunched the Honda's trunk into the back seat. Fortunately, the lady in the Honda was not hurt. Soon, a police car arrived.

Happily, it was Officer Murphy, who just happened to regularly serve as an usher at Sunday Mass. Officer Murphy immediately recognized Father McDuffy and surveyed the scene. Not that Officer Murphy feared for his soul, but he did ask Father McDuffy: "Father now, Jesus, Mary, and Joseph. Sure look now. I haven't a baldy notion how the lovely lass managed to back into your van so powerful. Wind your neck in whilst I dooter over and give the lovely lass a ticket."

NO CAN DO

A cop pulls a driver over for crossing the yellow line and then almost driving into a ditch. He tells the suspect to blow into a breathalyzer: "No can do, officer. I'm an asthmatic. I would get an asthma attack if I blew into that tube". The cop responds: "OK then, I'll take a urine sample". "No can do, officer. "I am a diabetic. I will get low blood sugar if I lose fluids". Impatiently, the cop says: "All right, then we will take a blood sample". The guy responds: "No can do that either, officer, I'm a hemophiliac. If I give blood, I can't stop the bleeding, and I will bleed to death". Finally, the exasperated cop says: "OK, then just walk straight on this white line". The guy replied: "No can do that either, officer". The cop says: "Why not?" The guy says: "Because I'm drunk as a skunk!"

TOTAL FEAR

A fellow bought a new Dodge Viper. He hit the I-10 interstate and blasted down the road. Faster and faster, to 150 MPH. But a cop had a Dodge Demon, and kept right up, lights flashing. The guy thought to himself: "This is crazy. I am a grandpa." He pulled over the waited for the cop. The trooper sauntered up to his Viper and said: "You gave me a good run for my money fellow. But I retire tomorrow, and if you can give me one great excuse for speeding like that which I have never heard before, I may let you go." The gentleman thought for a moment and said: "Years ago, my wife ran off with a State Trooper. I thought you were bringing her back." With a smile, the trooper said: "Have a good day, sir."

CHAPTER ELEVEN.

MECHANICS AND MIRTH

Everyone reading this book has dealt with mechanics. From them, some of us get no respect (like Rodney Dangerfield). Some of us don't trust them, over pay them, ridicule them, and some of us admire them. Whatever your experience, we have a joke for it.

RODNEY DANGERFIELD'S CAR GETS NO RESPECT

"Last week I told my mechanic, 'I keep thinking about suicide.' He told me from now on I have to pay for repairs in advance. My crummy old car was stolen. The thief sent a ransom note; it said: 'I want two thousand dollars or I'll bring it back!' I'll tell ya', my wife and I, we don't think alike. She donates money to the homeless, and I donate money to mechanics. My crummy old car…the mechanic told me: 'I'm very sorry. We did everything we could…but we were able to fix it.' My crummy old car, it has more vertical miles on it than horizontal miles…it's always on a lift! My wife isn't very bright. The other day she was at the store, and just as she was heading for our car, someone stole it! I said: 'Did you see the guy that did it?' She said, 'No, but I got the license plate number of your car as he drove it away.' I came from a real tough neighborhood. On my street, the kids take hubcaps - from moving cars! I saw a guy rotate my tires…from my car to his! My wife had her driver's test the other day. She got 8 out of 10. The other 2 guys jumped clear. My wife is a terrible driver, she once hit a deer. It was in a zoo! There is a pair of shoes hanging on the rear-view mirror. They belong to the last guy she ran over. My wife wanted sex in the back seat of the car and she asked me to drive! My wife felt romantic, so I took her to a drive-in movie. I spent the whole night trying to find out which car she was in."

Rodney Dangerfield, 1921-2004. No Respect by Rodney Dangerfield and Eric Teitelbaum, 1995; It's Not Easy Being Me: A Lifetime of No Respect but Plenty of Sex and Drugs by Rodney Dangerfield, 2005, and three YouTube Videos. These one-liner jokes are extracted from a variety of the above sources and were re-arranged by the author.

WHAT'S IN A NAME?

The senior mechanic yelled at his young trainee Vincent whenever he made the smallest mistake. "It's just something I do, so don't take it personal," he told young Vincent. But the kid replied: "If it's not personal, then why do you use my name?"

ROAD SERVICE

Road Service: "Just Relax. I'll have your flat tire changed in five minutes".

Driver: "How much will this cost me?"

Road Service: "It'll be $25."

Driver: "That much for five minutes?"

Road Service: "Well, if you prefer, I can take it off very slowly".

HIGH RATES

A man walks into an auto repair shop with two questions and inquired about the mechanic's rate of $150 for a simple oil change. "$50 for two questions," replied the mechanic. "Isn't that awfully steep?" asked the man. "Yes, the mechanic replied, "and what was your second question?"

MURPHY'S TEN LAWS FOR AUTO AFICIONADOS

"1. The largest vehicle always has the right of way.

2. When your car breaks down and it is a small repair, the mechanic has to remove the engine to get to that part.

3. When you take your car to a mechanic because it makes a funny sound you will not be able to demonstrate it for the mechanic nor will you be able to describe it.

4. If you're working under the hood of a car and drop something, it will always roll under the middle of the car and just out of reach.

5. The temperature of vinyl seat covers is inversely proportional to the length of your skirt or shorts.

6. Your car keys are always in the pocket of the hand that is fullest.

7. The louder the car alarm, the more likely everyone but the owner will hear it.

8. The oldest or cheapest vehicle has automatic right of way.

9. The vehicle with the largest driver has automatic right of way.

10. The vehicle with the most firearms on board (either factual or suspected) has automatic right of way."

These ten laws above selected from www.murphys-laws.com, Murphy's laws site: All the laws of Murphy in one place. Website is maintained by EricTheCarGuy.com. Eric cites the personal email address source for each "law", of which there are over 75. These are 10 of the best.

MURPHY'S SIX LAWS FOR JEEPS

"1. There's always a parking space when driving a 4 x 4.

2. Mud pools are always deeper then they appear.

3. The winch of a 4X4 is always just a little too short to reach a good hold.

4. There's never a tree around when you're stuck in the mud.

5. Mud tends to go where you do not want it to go.

6. Your snorkel is always that one inch to short when it comes down to taking a dive."

These six laws above selected from www.murphys-laws.com, Murphy's laws site: All the laws of Murphy in one place. Website is maintained by EricTheCarGuy.com. Eric cites the personal email address source for each "law", of which there are over 75. These are the 6 best.

BEING USEFUL

An auto mechanic had been in an insane asylum for some years but had improved to the point that the psychologists thought he was probably safe to return to society. At his final interview before being released, he was asked by the doctors what he would do. "I might teach shop at a vocational rehab institution," he suggested. "Or, I might run a tow truck at night to help stranded motorists," he said. "I might even write a book for mechanically-challenged dummies to help them repair their own cars," he said with a smile. "And if that does not work, I can always go back to being a carburetor!"

MOTTO

The mechanic had a big sign saying: WE OPERATE A CASH BUSINESS. (They get the cash, and you get the business).

CHARGED WITH BATTERY

Did you hear about the Die Hard mechanic who was arrested? He was charged with battery!

CONCENTRATE

Q. Why was the dumb mechanic staring at the orange juice container?

A. Because it said "concentrate".

GOING OUT WITH A BANG

A terrific explosion occurred in the Western Auto repair shop, and once all the mess had been cleaned up, an inquiry began. Ross the parts guy was asked to give a statement. "Okay Ross," said the investigator, "you were near the scene – what happened? "Well, it's like this. Greg was in the garage, and I saw him with a welding torch welding up an exhaust system right next to the car's gas tank." The investigator said, in stunned horror, "How long had he been with the shop?" "About 20 years, sir." said Ross. Astonished, the investigator said, "Twenty years in the shop, then he goes and torches a gas tank. I'd have thought it would have been the last thing he'd have done." "It was, sir," Ross replied.

A REAL GAS

When Roland started working at the gas station, he saw his boss drop a long wooden measuring stick into the underground gas tank. "What would happen if I threw a lit match into the underground tank?", Roland joked. "It would go out," his boss said with a straight face. "Really?" Roland asked, surprised to hear that. "Is there oxygen deficiency down there or a high-tech safety device that would extinguish the match before the fumes ignited?" "No," Roland's boss said: "The force from the explosion would blow out the match."

TOUGH QUESTION FOR ROLAND

Roland came home early from his part-time job at a gas station. His friend asked why he was home so soon this afternoon, since he usually worked until 8pm. Roland said: "They let me off early because I was the only one who could answer a tough question." "Oh, really? What was the question?", Teko asked. Roland replied: "Who filled a customer's diesel car gas tank with gasoline?"

DEAD BATTERIES

Did you hear about the guy who gave all his dead batteries away to strangers? They were ... free of charge.

TIME ENOUGH?

Arnold, who was a car guy with lots of cars, went into a coma for ten years. He awoke to his joyous wife. They were cleaning out his drawer and he came across a receipt from Big Daddy's Texaco. The date stamped was ten years ago. He forgot to pick up a car from a brake job of a decade ago! Arnold drove straight to the repair shop, which was still in business. With a straight face, he handed the ticket to Big Daddy behind the counter, and said, "I'm Arnold, and here to pick up my car from the brake job." With a straight face, Big Daddy said, "Just a minute. I'll have to look for this." He disappeared onto the back lot, but two minutes later, Big Daddy called out: "Here it is!" "No kidding?", Arnold called back. "That's terrific! Who would have thought it would still be here after all this time." Big Daddy came back to Arnold, empty-handed. "Sorry neighbor. It won't be ready until Monday," he said calmly.

DO I HAVE YOUR EAR?

There were two Mopar fellows working on a 383 block after hours in a garage, when the first fellow got too close to the rotating engine fan blade and got his ear cut off. It fell in the grease pit, and he got down on his knees and started looking around for his ear. The other fellow jumped in the pit and said he would help the first fellow search for the ear. "Here it is, I found it," said the second fellow. The first fellow took it, looked at it carefully and said: "That's not mine, keep looking, mine had a yellow pencil behind it," as he tossed it away.

THE SLACKER

A large Toyota dealership hired a new top manager. He was stern and authoritative and disliked lazy employees with a passion. He spotted a guy sitting on a chair, doing nothing. Meanwhile, all the mechanics in the shop seemed busy. The manager asked the guy in the chair: "How much money do you make a week?" "I earn $150 a week. What's it to you?" The manager was insulted, went to the payroll office, and handed the guy $1,000 in cash and said: "Here's your severance. You are fired. Don't ever come back." The guy scurried away. The manager then said loudly for all the mechanics to hear: "So what did that slacker do here?" The head mechanic from across the room said, "Nothing. He was the Domino's pizza delivery guy."

BOSS VS. MECHANIC'S TEN-ITEM CHECKLIST

Boss: Test drive OK but cruise control not working.

Mechanic: Cruise control not installed on this car.

Boss: Something loose behind dash.

Mechanic: Something tightened behind dash.

Boss: Dead bugs on windshield.

Mechanic: Live bugs on backorder.

Boss: Evidence of leak on right front brake drum.

Mechanic: Evidence removed.

Boss: Radio volume unbelievably loud.

Mechanic: Radio volume set to more believable level.

Boss: Suspected crack in windshield.

Mechanic: Suspect you're right.

Boss: Engine seems to be missing.

Mechanic: Opened hood, found engine.

Boss: Engine runs funny.

Mechanic: Happy engine warned to be more serious.

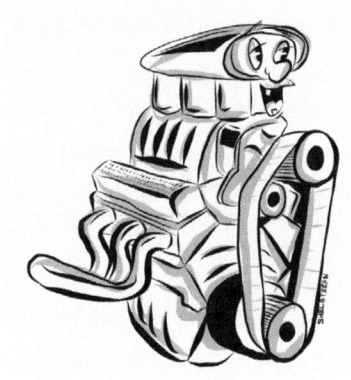

Boss: Mouse in trunk.

Mechanic: Put cat in trunk.

Boss: Loud banging noise coming from transmission. Sounds like a madman with a hammer.

Mechanic: Took hammer away from madman.

POEM: PRAISING THE MECHANIC

His fingernails show grease, oil and wear.

But that's part of his job.

And so his blood does tend to boil at times.

When we act like a snob.

He takes an awful lot of bunk.

But keeps on hanging' in.

He still works on our greasy parts.

And makes them Fords purr once again.

As our Fords start to cough and choke, he says with a smirk.

Stand back, folks, and let a real surgeon work.

---Calvin Stokes

GOOD OL' BOY MECHANIC

When my husband and I arrived at the repair shop to pick up our car, we were told that the keys had been accidentally locked in it. We went to the service department and found a goofy-looking mechanic working feverishly trying to pick the lock from outside the driver's side door. As I watched from the passenger's side, I instinctively tried the right door handle and discovered it unlocked. "Hey," I announced to the guy, "It's open!" "I know," answered the mechanic. "I already got that side."

WIRING HARNESS

A man ordered a wiring harness for his old Ford...The harness arrived in 97 pieces! The instructions said that it could be put together in an hour. However, it took the man two days to figure out the harness. Finally, when it was all put together, he wrote a check, cut it into 97 pieces and mailed it off to the wiring company.

TRUCK WON'T RUN

Customer with disabled truck, to mechanic Bob, "May I ask you a question?" Paul, the mechanic: "Sure, what is it?" Bob: "An interrogative sentence, and expression of inquiry, an expression of doubt...but that's not important. Let's find out why your truck won't run."

TWO ENGINE IMPRESSIONS

Customer question: "Can you two mechanics give me your impression of my engine?"

Mechanic A: "Sure! Clunk! Clunk! Bang! Grind! Clunk! Clunk!"

Mechanic B: "Sorry, I don't do engine impressions."

CHEVY TRUCK WON'T START

As mechanic bends over engine compartment, looking for a reason why Chevy truck won't start...

Customer: "What's it look like?"

Mechanic: "A greasy small block Chevy engine that won't start..."

COUNT DOWN

A guy has a knocking motor and drives the car to his mechanic to listen. The mechanic says: "I'm afraid I have some bad news. Your motor's dying and it doesn't have much time." "Oh no, that's terrible! How long has it got?", the man asks. "10..." says the mechanic. "10 what?!? Months? Weeks? Days? Hours? Seconds? What?? "Asks the man. The mechanic replied: "9...8...7...6..."

PARTS

Letter to a parts supplier: "Send me a water pump; if it's any good, I will send you a check."

Parts supplier Reply: "Send me the check. If it's any good, we will send you the water pump."

CRAPPY FIX

A nerd pushes his BMW into a gas station. He tells the mechanic it died. After the mechanic works on it for a few minutes, it is idling smoothly. He says, "What was the fix?" The mechanic replies, "Just crap in the carburetor." The nerd says, "How often do I have to do that?"

GOOD TRADE

A guy walks into the Western Auto and says: "How about a gas cap for a Yugo." Kevin the parts counter guy said: "Okay, sounds like a fair trade."

THE BUSINESSMAN AND THE BODY MAN

A businessman was at a body shop, and complimented the body man on the fine quality of his work. But the body man only worked 25 hours per week at his trade. The businessman asked why didn't he work at it 50-60 hours and make twice as much money. The body man said that 25 hours a week was all the time he needed to work to support his family's immediate needs. The businessman then asked the man how he spent the rest of his time. The body man said, "I sleep late, fish a little, play with my children, take romantic siestas with my wife, and work on my classic car in my spare time." The businessman scoffed, "I am a Harvard MBA and could help you. You should spend more time doing body work and, with the proceeds, buy a bigger shop. With the proceeds from the bigger shop, you hire more men, get a chain of body shops, and then run your expanding enterprise. The body man asked "But how long will all this take?" To which the businessman replied, "15-20 years." "But what after that?" asked the body man. The businessman laughed, and said, "That's the best part! When the time is right, you would sell your company stock to the public. You'll become very rich, you will make millions!" "Millions?" replied the body man. "Then what?"

The businessman said, "Then you would retire. You could sleep late, fish a little, play with your grandkids, take romantic siestas with your wife, and work on your classic car in your spare time."

(adapted from www.personalmba.com)

FOURTEEN MISLEADING CAR AD CLAIMS. THEY REALLY MEAN...

1. Rough condition...too bad to lie about

2. Parts car...beyond repair

3. Immaculate...recently washed

4. Engine quiet...if you use 90-weight oil

5. Needs minor overhaul...needs engine

6. Needs major overhaul...phone the junkyard

7. Burns no oil...it all leaked out

8. Rebuilt engine...cleaned the spark plugs

9. Drive it away...I live on a hill

10. Drive it anywhere...within 10 miles

11. Desirable classic...no one wants it

12. Rare classic...no one wanted it even when it was new

13. Stored 20 years...in a farmer's field

14. Ran when stored...won't start

SHIRLEY, I AM SERIOUS

Mechanic (to Customer): "The cost to fix your old car's transmission will be $1,300."

Customer: "Surely you can't be serious!"

Mechanic: "I *am* serious. And *don't* call me Shirley!"

PISSED AND BROKE

Mechanic Gary of Annapolis went for a drive in his 1948 Ford F-3 and the motor went "clunk, clunk, clunk" then shuddered and died. He raised the hood and looked in anger at the motor. His buddy Jack drove by and stopped, asking: "What's the problem?" "Piston broke", Gary muttered. "Me too," says Jack.

RIGHT OR LEFT?

DRIVER TO MECHANIC: "What is wrong with my car?"

MECHANIC: "On the right side, there's nothing left. On the left side, there's nothing right.

GOOD DEAL

Becky drives Carol to pick up her car from the mechanic. Becky asks, "Everything OK with your car now?" Carol replies, "Yes, at first I had concerns that my mechanic might try to snooker me, but I was pleased when he said that all I needed was $75 worth of blinker fluid."

THE MECHANIC WHO LOVED 104 OCTANE GAS

The old mechanic liked to run 104 octane gas in his truck and race car. He thought its benefits to be so great that he used 104 octane gas (instead of milk) in his cereal every morning. He lived to age 90 and was cremated according to his wishes. There is a flaming 20 foot deep hole where the Crispy's Crematorium once was.

PUZZLED SERVICE MANAGER

An unsatisfied customer went back to Western Tire and Auto to complain to the Service Manager: "Craig," he said to the Service Manager, "you put on four new tires, but two of them are black walls and two are raised letter whites. What gives?" Craig was puzzled: "I don't understand. Yesterday another customer complained about the very same thing."

ADDICTED MECHANIC

Have you heard about the mechanic who was addicted to power steering fluid? He was sure he was *right* that if he *left* power steering fluid alone for a while that he could indulge in brake fluid. That he knew he could stop anytime.

POOR MECHANIC

At the service station a little boy told the owner: "When I grow up, I'm going to give you some money." "Well, thank you," the mechanic replied, "But why?" "Because my daddy says you're one of the poorest mechanics we've ever had."

MECHANIC'S BEST FRIEND

The mechanic was talking to his customer about his dog, Rover: "Every day Rover brings me Alfa Romeo parts. One day, a door handle. Next day, a bumper guard. Then, a hood ornament and a windshield wiper blade." "Wow," said the customer, "what a bright and useful dog!" The mechanic replied: "Aww, he's not so smart. I don't even *have* an Alfa Romeo!"

CHAPTER TWELVE

DOCTOR, IT HURTS HERE...

All aficionados ultimately must deal with doctors, druggists, and nurses. How can these encounters possibly be funny? No problem when we tickle your funny bone.

QUACK TURNS DOCTOR

A travelling medicine show quack got bored with fleecing rubes at Carlyle with fake arthritis medicine. He ordered an MD degree from a diploma mill and decided to prey upon gullible car guys. He changed his name to Dr. Quack. He opened a medical clinic and put up a sign up that read:

"DR. QUACK'S CLINIC. TREATMENTS, JUST $300. IF NOT CURED, GET BACK $600 REFUND."

A savvy old car guy was suspicious and decided to try Dr. Quack.

Car guy: "Dr. Quack, I have lost the ability to taste. Do you have a remedy for me?"

Dr. Quack: "Yes, I do. Here is special medicine from bottle #101 and a teaspoon. I will now put into the spoon a spoonful of sugar in it to help the medicine go down."

Car guy: (Tasting it) Yukkk!!! -- "This tastes like gasoline!"

Dr. Quack: Congratulations! You've got your taste back. That will be $300." The car guy thought he had been fleeced, so he went back a few days later to Dr. Quack to get even.

Car guy: I must have Alzheimer's Disease. I cannot recall anything.

Dr. Quack: "I can fix this. Here is an eyedropper with special medicine from bottle #101. Swallow it now."

Car guy: "Hold on there, Dr. Quack. I remember #101. That was gasoline!"

Dr. Quack: "Wonderful! Your memory is cured. That will cost you another $300."

The car guy has now lost $600 to Dr. Quack, but he tries again in a few days.

Car guy: "My eyesight has become totally blurred. I can't see well enough to drive my old car."

Dr. Quack: "Well, I am completely stumped. I have no cure for vision loss. I owe you a $600 refund." Here is your cash. (Dr. Quack gave him a $1 and $5 bill).

Car guy: "But this is only a $5 bill and a $1 bill, not $600!"

Dr. Quack: "How wonderful! Your eyesight problem is cured. That will cost you another $300."

CALL ME ANYTHING

Doctor to not-too-smart doorman at posh hotel: "Quick! Call me a taxi!"

Doorman to Doctor: "Well, OK, Doc, you're a taxi."

CALL FOR HELP

A doctor was waiting outside his hotel when a careless taxi driver ran over his foot, and he cried out for help. The Doorman called (wait for it) a toe truck!

BACKATCHA

Dooley was being evaluated for mental problems and was asked by the doctor, "If a train was coming down the track after you, what would you do?" Dooley replied, "I would get in my red '55 Ford Victoria and speed away!" The doctor then asked, "Where did you get that car from?" Dooley replied, "The same place you got that train!"

MECHANIC VS. M.D.

A doctor said to his car mechanic, "You charge more per hour than we get paid for medical care." "Yeah, Doc, but you only have two models. They are standard. We mechanics have new and updated models every single year."

TRANQUIL MOM

The teenage boy had just gotten his fifth ticket for speeding. His mother was advised by her psychiatrist: "You don't need to be upset and worried about your son. I suggest you take these tranquilizers daily. They will reduce your tension and anxiety." On her next visit, the psychiatrist asked, "Have the tranquilizers calmed you?" "Yes" the mother answered. "And how is your son now?", the psychiatrist asked. "What son?" she replied. *(adapted from www.jokes4all.net)*

SIX MONTHS LEFT

Three good ol' boys were engaged in a conversation of what each would do if the doctor said he had just six months to live. Steve said: "I would bust loose, sell my house and old cars, and have girls, girls, and more girls." Harry said: "If my doctor said I had only six months to live, the first thing I would do is I would buy a Corvette, a '57 Chevy, and a '55 Cadillac." John said: "If my doctor said I had only six months to live, the first thing I would do would be to consult another doctor."

(adapted from www.sentineleffectwordpress.com)

A CASE OF SHINGLES

A carpenter named Yates drove his pickup to the doctor's office, and the receptionist asked him what he had. Yates said, "Shingles." So she took down his height, weight, a complete medical history and told Yates to wait in the examining room. A half-hour later a different nurse came in and asked Yates what he had. Yates said, "Shingles." So she gave Yates a blood test, a blood pressure test, an electrocardiogram, and told Yates to strip only to the waist and wait for the doctor. Yates did as instructed and took off his pants. A minute later, the doctor came in and asked Yates why he was half- naked and what he had. Yates said, "Shingles." The doctor said, "What?" Yates said, "Shingles." The doctor said, "Where? I don't see anything below your waist. Where?" Yates said, "Outside in the truck. Where do you want them?"

(adapted from www.malesurvivor.org)

DUMB QUESTION

Attorney: "Doctor, how many auto accident autopsies have you performed on dead people?"

Doctor: "All of them, the live ones put up too much of a fight."

DONE IN, TOO SOON

Lester worked under old cars and in his garden so much that he felt like his body had gotten tired and flabby. So he got his doc's permission to join a fitness club, and started exercising. He decided to take an aerobics class for seniors. He bent, stretched, clenched, squatted, and pulled for an hour. But, when he finally got his leotards on, the class was over! Done in, too soon.

(adapted from www.homeyra.wordpress.com)

TAMPONS FOR BOYS?

Two very young boys walked into a pharmacy one day, picked out a box of tampons and proceeded to the checkout counter. The clerk at the counter asked the older boy, "Son, how old are you?" "Eight," the boy replied. The clerk continued, "Do you know what these are used for?" The boy replied, "Not exactly, but they aren't for me. They're for my little brother. He's four. We saw on TV that if you use these, you would be able to ride a bike and a snowmobile. Right now, he can't do either one."

(adapted from www.adultmatchdoctor.com)

THE RX PRESCRIPTION

Art, a 76-year-old man, had tired blood and went to the doctor to get a physical and maybe some "vitamins". A few days later, the doctor saw Art driving down the street in a red Dodge Viper with a gorgeous young lady on his arm. A couple of days later the doctor spoke to Art and said, "You look like you are doing great, aren't you?" Art replied, "Just doing what you said: get a hot mamma and be cheerful." Shocked, the doctor said, "I didn't say that. I said, 'You've got a heart murmur. Be careful'".

BAD NEWS & GOOD NEWS

Calvin had been in a terrible auto accident. After two days in a coma, he woke up and found the surgeon standing beside his hospital bed. "I have bad and good news for you," said the surgeon. "The bad news is that I cut off your healthy leg by mistake." "Oh, no!" exclaimed Calvin. "Now tell me the good part." "The good part is that your bad leg healed up!"

GOIN' LIKE 60

Two paramedics were dispatched to check on an elderly man who had become disoriented. They decided to take him to the hospital for evaluation. Along the way, with siren going, they questioned the man to determine his level of aware-ness. Leaning close, one asked: "Sir, do you know what we're doing right now?" The old man slowly looked out the ambulance window. "Oh," he replied, "I'd say about 60, maybe 65."

(adapted from www.crochetnmore.com)

DON'T DO DAT!

A guy drove in a demolition derby race and the medic at the track told him that his arm was broken in three places. He went to the doctor, who admonished him: "Don't go to those places!"

PHOTO FIX

Becky, a professional photographer, was in an auto accident. The doctor said: "Your X-ray shows you've got a broken arm and a broken ankle." Becky replied, "Don't worry; I've already fixed them with Photoshop."

AUTO BODY PROBLEMS

A man went into his psychiatrist's office and said, "Doc, you have to help me!" "What seems to be the problem?", asked the doctor. "Well, every night I dream that I'm a car part. The other night I dreamed I was a Chevy Impala fender. Another night I dreamed I was a Plymouth Fury door. Last night I dreamed I was a Dodge Duster hood. What does this mean?" The doctor gave the matter some serious consideration as his patient waited anxiously for the determination. "Relax," said the doctor, "You're just having an auto-body experience."

GOOD OL' BOY'S PAIN

A fellow entered a demolition derby and got injured and went to the doctor. He complained that his body hurt wherever he touched it. Said the doctor: "Show me." The old boy took his finger, pushed on his stomach and screamed in pain, and then he pushed his elbow and screamed even more. He pushed his knee and screamed; likewise, he pushed his ankle and winced in pain. Everywhere he touched made him holler. The doctor said, "Your finger is broken."

CHECKUP

This well-aged ex-military guy drove his Vintage Jeep to his VA hospital for a checkup. The doctor asked him: "When was the last time you made love???" "1945" he replied. "That long ago?" quizzed the doctor? The military guy replied: "Not so bad, only three hours ago...now it's only 21-15!"

CRANKY

Hear about the cranky, cantankerous car guy who got killed in a car wreck? The autopsy was refused by the patient!

SURGEONS PREFER...

"Five surgeons taking a coffee break—

1st surgeon says: "Accountants are the best to operate on because when you open them up, everything inside is numbered."

2nd surgeon says: "Nah, librarians are the best. Everything inside them is in alphabetical order."

3rd surgeon says: "Try electricians, man! Everything inside THEM is color coded!"

4th surgeon says: "I prefer lawyers. They're heartless, spineless, gutless and their heads and their butts are interchangeable."

To which the 5th surgeon, who has been quietly listening to the conversations, says: "I like old car restorers...they always understand when you have a few parts left over at the end."

(adapted from www.polylith.com; www.jokesgalore.com)

OLD CAR COLLECTOR

A pudgy old car collector had a heart attack, and was rushed by ambulance to the hospital for heart surgery. While in a coma, he sees God, and asks: "Will I die?" God replies: "No, you will live another 30 years." So the pudgy fellow gets liposuction, a tummy tuck, plastic surgery on his turkey neck, and hair implants. He finally exits the hospital looking 20 years younger, but is immediately run over by a school bus and killed. Again he sees God, and complains: "God, you said I had 30 more years to live." God replies: "Sorry, I didn't recognize you."

DOCTOR DARKLY

A man woke up in a hospital after a floor jack fell on his feet, and his feet went numb. He shouted, "Doctor, doctor I can't feel my legs!" The doctor replies, "I know you can't—I've cut off your arms!"

BETTER PRESCRIPTION

An older gentleman goes to his favorite doctor for advice. He says: "Doc, I've got my weight down, I take vitamins, I've had plastic surgery, I take Viagra, and there is a beautiful young woman who I am trying to attract. But I am having no luck at all. Can you please recommend any special devices which I should try next?" The doctor thought about it and recommended to him with a smile; "I can only suggest two things--the ATM machine and a new Corvette. Both should help you get results."

DIM PROGNOSIS FOR FRANK

An old fellow, Frank, is feeling tired and out-of-sorts, and decides to go to the doctor. His wife Nikki insists on going with him. Frank meets privately with the doctor and tells the doctor about his life and hobbies. The doctor does tests, and tells him he will mail him the results. Frank goes to the car, but Nikki goes back to talk with the doctor privately. "Tell me the hard cold truth, doctor," she said. The doctor said: "I will be entirely frank with you about Frank", as he chuckles privately. Frank is actually in very good health for his age. His tests are all normal, but his life is in the doldrums." Nikki replies: "Wow, anything I can do to help him?" The doctor says: "Yes. Fix him a nice supper every night. Make love a couple of times each week. Furthermore, he loves his old car hobby and his orange and white 1956 Mercury. Visit with him in the garage, hand him his tools, and bring him a beer now and then. Go with him on poker nights and tell him it's OK if he loses a few bucks. Also, go to car shows with him, even if riding in the old Mercury musses your hair in the wind." "Thank you doctor," as she leaves to see Frank at the car. Frank says to Nikki: "What's the verdict?" Nikki looks down in a despondent manner, then raises her head to look at Frank, and with a mischievous smirk she says: "You're gonna die." *(adapted from www.teacherjoe.us)*

CHAPTER THIRTEEN

CRUISERS, THEIR FAMILIES AND FRIENDS

Auto enthusiasts interact daily with their families and friends. Enjoying humor with people close to us enriches our lives. Prepare to laugh and be enriched!

ASSASSIN SCREENING

In the year 2025, a top secret old car organization was formed to assassinate politicians who pass "crusher laws" and "clunker legislation". The group was called "OURS"—"Old Ugly Rattletrap Survivors." The group had an opening for an assassin. So the assassin recruiters bring an applicant to the door and hand him a gun. "We must know that you will follow instructions no matter what the circumstances," they explained. "Inside you will find your wife tied to a chair. Take this gun and kill her." The man looked a bit shocked, but nevertheless he took the gun and went in the room. All was quiet for about 5 minutes, and then the door opened. The man came out of the room with tears in his eyes. "I thought about shooting her; I just couldn't pull the trigger and shoot my wife. I guess I'm not the right man for the job." "No," the assassin guys replied, "You are not loyal to OURS. Leave this place." Next, they have a female left to test. Again they lead her to a door to the room and hand her a gun: "We must be sure that you will do what we say. This is your test. Inside you will find your husband tied to a chair. Take this gun and shoot him." The woman took the pistol and the door closed. The group heard the pistol firing six shots. Then they heard screaming, crashing, banging on the walls. The woman emerged from the room and said, "You guys didn't tell me the pistol was loaded with blanks! I had to beat him to death with the chair."

(adapted from www.funnygrins.com)

INSIGHT

A young man was blind since birth, but told his friend not to feel bad for him. "Every girl I date is a #10, and I never get traffic tickets."

SUPER SALE

Doby's Western Auto store had a super sale starting at 8:00 a.m. on Saturday... "SIX QUARTS OF OIL WITH FILTER, JUST $5". A bunch of guys lined up at 7:30 a.m., when Doby tried to work his way to the front of the line. Guys like Pugnacious Paul, Bruiser Bob, Wicked Warren, and Reckless Rich just pushed him to the back of the line, over and over, saying to him: "Don't you know we're just going to push you to the back again?" "Maybe", said Doby, "But if you don't let me to the front, I'll never be able to open the store!"

SHARKS OF A FEATHER

A banker, a doctor, and a used car salesman went swimming in water which they did not know was infested with sharks. The sharks quickly gobbled up the banker and the doctor. But a ferocious-looking shark locked his teeth tightly together and gently pushed the used car salesman safely to shore. "Why did you give me such special consideration?" asked the salesman. The shark grunted: "Professional courtesy."

STINKY HEATER

Dear Big Bird Tech Advisor:

Last year, I bought my vintage 1965 Ford Thunderbird Landau with a warrantee from Cool Classic Cars dealership. This winter, with the heater on, the warm air started to stink. I took it back to the car dealership, and they found a dead rat in the heater duct. They want to charge me for removing the rat. I said that the rat was in the car when I bought it, so I should not have to pay. They said it came from my garage. Who is right?

Signed, TBird Guy

Dear TBird Guy:

First of all, was it a rat rod? (HA HA). If not, here is how to find out for sure. Get a description of the rat. If it was wearing plaid pants, white shoes, a white belt, and played music on a CD, it is a dealership rat. If, on the other hand, the rat had greasy pants and an eight-track tape playing 60's tunes, it probably came from your garage.

Signed, Big Bird Tech Advisor

QUICK MARRIAGE

A man and a woman had a torrid romance and married. After three days, the next morning, she awoke to find her husband dressing. "Dear," he said, "We married so quickly that I never told you that on Saturdays I like to first go to a car show and then go golfing." "Darling," she said, "That's OK. We married so fast that I never told you that I'm a hooker." The fellow said, "No problem. Easily fixed. You just hold the golf club like such..."

BETTY'S ANTICIPATION

Betty awoke with a start the morning of her 30th wedding anniversary with Bob. Bob asked: "What's the matter?" Betty said: "I had a dream that you gave me a new Corvette for an anniversary present. It was red and had an automatic transmission so I could drive it. What could it mean?" Bob said: "I have a feeling you'll know tonight, when I get home." That evening, when Bob returned from work, he gave her a flowery anniversary card and a medium-small package to unwrap. Thinking it was a key to her new car, with great anticipation, she ripped open the gift paper. It was a book, Understanding Your Dreams.

CASH FOR THE TRIP

Skip, Paul, and Bob were mourning the loss of a car collector friend. Skip said, "As you well know, I am thrifty, but there is a Maryland tradition that if one places a bit of money in the casket so that it may be buried with the body, it will ease the way into the next world. I will place a fifty dollar bill in the casket with him." "Well," Paul said, "I, too, will contribute fifty dollars." Bob said: "I agree, I, too, will contribute $50." And pulling out his checkbook, he quickly made out a check for $150 dollars, placed it on the dead man's breast, and took the two $50 bills as change.

CONTROLLED ANGER

WIFE: Why don't you fight back when I get angry at you? How do you handle it?

HUSBAND: I detail the engine on my classic Mustang.

WIFE: How does that help?

HUSBAND: I use your toothbrush.

KILL ANYONE?

The young boy was spending a Sunday afternoon with his grandpa. Looking at pictures of his grandpa in his military uniform, the boy asked, "Grandpa, did you ever kill anyone in the war?" Grandpa replied: "No champ, I never did." The boy replied: "That's a good thing." Said Grandpa: "You're telling me. I was an ambulance driver!"

TEN EXERCISES WHICH CAR GUYS SHOULD AVOID

1. Jumping on a tire to break the bead off the rim

2. Wading through paperwork to add up restoration expenses

3. Running around in circles looking for a dropped nut

4. Pushing your luck when you are low on gas

5. Playing games on your Apple I-10 phone in heavy traffic

6. Spinning your wheels in the mud

7. Adding fuel to a carb which backfires

8. Beating your head against a brick wall when your car won't start on the morning of a car show

9. Climbing the walls without a soft landing pad below

10. Beating your own drum when your car gets a trophy and your friend's car does not

EIGHT MORE EXERCISES FOR CAR GUYS TO AVOID

1. Jumping to conclusions about why your motor misses after you do a tune up

2. Grasping at straws after you replace a light bulb and it still flickers

3. Fishing for compliments after you switch from black walls to wide whites

4. Throwing your weight around at the car club meeting

5. Passing the buck when you are the one who did substandard bodywork before you had your car painted

6. Running with scissors to cut a loose thread hanging from the trunk

7. Failing to pay your car club dues on time

8. Dragging your heels when adding air to your tires

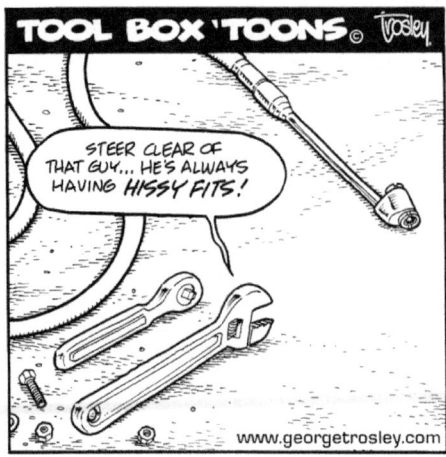

VICTORIA MOTOR OIL

While experimenting in his garage one day, Messy Mike accidentally got some Victoria Motor Oil on his finger and he licked it off. "Hmmmm...Not bad!" he exclaimed. So he took a few big glugs from the can, and he felt fine that night, and fine the next day. So the next day, Messy Mike took his can of Victoria Motor Oil over to his friends' garages, Valiant Vincent and Big Bo. Valiant Vincent tried the oil and liked it. But Big Bo refused it, thinking it might be deadly. Soon thereafter, Sexy Lexi came by, and wanted to try some. She loved it. So immediately Big Bo also took a few swigs and found that he actually liked it. Valiant Vincent took Big Bo aside and privately asked him: "How is it that you're drinking the motor oil today when you wouldn't touch the stuff before Sexy Lexi came?" Big Bo explained: "It's not what you think. I figured that it would be better for me to be found dead with Messy Mike and Valiant Vincent than to explain Sexy Lexi sick or dead in my garage!"

HAPPINESS

Three car dignitaries were in a private jet on cross-country flight: Herman Firestone, inventor of the donut spare tire; Zastava Koral, inventor of the Yugo; and Ralph Nader, author of "Corvair: Unsafe at Any Speed." Firestone pulls out a $1,000 bill and says: "I'm going to throw this $1,000 bill out the window and make one American very happy." Not wanting to be outdone, Koral the Yugo guy says: "Hah! I will throw ten $100 bills out, and make ten Americans happy." Ralph Nader then opens his briefcase, counts out 1,000 one dollar bills, and smugly says: "I will now make 1,000 Americans happy!" The pilot overheard all of this bragging, and says: "I think I'll throw all three of you out and make 350 million Americans happy."

REALISTIC PHOTO

The Mom was proud of her son, who had just gotten his first car at age 17. She was trying to take a picture of her son with the car, posed with his father. "Let's try to make this look natural," she said. "Junior, put your arm around your Dad's shoulder." The Dad answered, "If you want it to look reallstic, why not have him put his hand on my wallet?"

DRIVES LIKE LIGHTNING

Ted and Bob were discussing their wives' driving styles. Ted noted that his wife drove so slow that he was always afraid they'd get hit from behind. Bob countered by saying, "My wife drives like lightning." "She drives fast?", asked Ted. Bob replied: "No, she hits trees and splits them!"

BORN ON THE 4TH OF JULY

All of his life, Dick from New Hampshire had heard stories of an amazing family tradition. It seems that his father and grandfather had all been able to drive their old cars across Lake Winnepesaka on their 21st birthday. On that day, they'd drive across the lake to a waterfront restaurant for their first legal drink. So when Dick's 21st birthday came around, he drove his old car to the lake, hit the gas, and immediately sank. Dick nearly drowned, but managed to swim to safety. Upset and confused, Dick went to see his grandmother, "Grandma, it's my 21st birthday, so why can't I drive across the lake like my father and his father?" Granny looked into Dick's eyes and said, "Because, dear Dick, your father and grandfather were born in January, you were born on July 4th?" *(Get it? The lake was frozen in January, but not in July!)*

WARNING

Dad is waxing his Cadillac. His 5-year-old son is holding a frog and says: "Dad, please don't ever put my frog in your trunk." Dad curiously says, "Why not?" The boy says, "Because—my pet python might eat him."

SHORT TIME LEFT

As her elderly husband's funeral service, the undertaker asked Gladys: "How old was your husband?" She replied: "As old as our Model T—98 years old. One year older than me." "So you're 97?", the undertaker commented. She responded sadly, "Hardly worth going home, is it?"

MORAL: COMPLAIN TO THE RICH

After trying a new shampoo for the first time, Morris mailed off an enthusiastic letter of approval to the manufacturer. Several weeks later he came home from work to find a large carton on the middle of the foyer floor. Inside were free samples of the many products the same company produced: soaps, detergents, toothpaste, and paper items...along with a "thank you" note from the manufacturer. "Well, what do you think?", asked his smiling wife, Ruth. "I think that next time," Morris replied, "I'm writing to the Ford Motor Company!"

(adapted from www.crochetmore.com)

A PEACEFUL DEATH

When I die, I want to die like my grandfather, who died in a lovely deep sleep, not like his screaming passenger in the front seat next to him.

A POEM: WHY OLD CARS BECOME OUR SPECIAL LADIES

1) Think about it. It's really quite easy.

2) They don't glare at us when our hands are all greasy.

3) They don't sulk and demand our attention.

4) They don't get angry and say things I can't mention.

5) They sit and wait for us with never a peep.

6) And no forgotten birthday will cause them to weep.

7) If you offer advice to your wife, she'll probably nix it.

8) But, if your car has a problem, she's happy when you fix it.

9) They're shiny and lovely just like the girls.

10) But never demand diamonds and pearls.

11) Oh, they both have demands, of that you can be sure.

12) But I think the ladies have a few hundred more.

13) So, if you read this with your wife, don't say you agree

14) Or, you'll probably be sleeping in your car, like me.

----Ray Idleman, Jr.

GOOD NEWS AND BAD NEWS

A woman phones up her husband at work for a chat...the husband answers and says, "I'm sorry dear, but I'm up to my neck in work today." The wife replies, "But I've got some good news and some bad news for you, dear." The husband says, "Okay, darling, but as I've got very little time, please give me just the good news." "Well," says the wife, "the air bag works."

FATHERS WON'T SAY FIVE THINGS

Here are five things you'll never hear anyone's father say:

1. Well how 'bout that? I'm lost! Looks like we'll have to stop and ask for directions.

2. You know Pumpkin, now that you're thirteen, you'll be ready for non-chaperoned car dates. Won't that be fun?

3. Here's a credit card and the keys to my new car. GO CRAZY!!!

4. Well, I don't know what's wrong with your car. Probably one of those doo-hickie thingies—you know—that makes it run or something. Just have it towed to the mechanic and pay whatever he asks.

5. Father's Day? Ah—don't worry about that—it's no big deal.

HIS REAL VALUE

The classic Ford owned by Bob and Tammy totally burned up after a gas tank leak got out of hand, and Tammy called the insurance company: "We had that car insured for thirty thousand and I want my money. The car is junk now," said Tammy to the insurance agent. "Whoa there just a minute, Tammy," said the agent, "it doesn't work quite like that. We will ascertain the value of the car and provide you with another one of its actual comparable worth." After a long pause, Tammy said: "In that case, I'd like to change the life insurance policy on my husband."

THE SEX OF FLIES

A woman walked into the garage to find her husband swatting flies. She asked him if he killed any. "Of course," he said, "Four males, two females." She asked: "How can you tell which is which?" He responded, "Four males were on my Plymouth Fury, and the two females were on the phone."

ARREST, OR A REST?

A boy and his father are playing with toy cars late one night. The father has the police car and pretends to pull over the car the boy is playing with. "Do you have a driver's license?", asks the father. "No," says the boy. "Are you resisting arrest?", he asks. The boy hesitates before he says: "No, I'm not sleepy yet." *(Get it...a rest?)*

FATHER'S DAY GIFT

This past Father's Day, my son gave me something I had wanted for years - the keys back to my own car!

MAP TORTURE

To torture my Dad, I would fold up the map wrong and stuff it back into his glove box. To really torture him, I would fold it up wrong right in front of him.

THE FARM GIRL

Jack, from Georgia, decided to go to a car show in Canada with his buddy, Bob. They took Jack's Land Cruiser and headed for the Canadian border. On that rainy night, they pulled into a nearby farmhouse and asked the attractive lady who answered the door if they could spend the night. The lady agreed, but she was recently widowed, and did not want to give reason for her neighbors to gossip. They could sleep for free in the barn. Her deceased husband's classic cars were still there. Come morning, the weather had cleared, and they were on their way to Canada. Nine months later, Jack got an unexpected letter from the attorney representing the widow. Jack quickly visited his friend Bob and asked, "Bob, do you remember that widow at the farm?" "Yes, I do." Jack continued: "Did you happen to get up in the middle of the night, go up to the house and were you extremely romantic with her?" "Yes," Bob said, a little embarrassed about being discovered. "I have to admit that I did." "And did you happen to use my name instead of telling her yours?" Bob's face turned red and he said, "Yeah, sorry Jack, I'm afraid I did. Why do you ask?" Jack said: "She just died and left me $100,000 and her husband's collection of classic Fords." *(You thought the ending would be different, didn't you?)*

(adapted from www.gameboomers.com)

UNFAIR FIGHT

Teenage grandson: "I got this title for Grandpa's 1957 Chevy Bel Air on his death-bed...he put up one heck of a fight for it!"

SAY AGAIN?

A husband asked his wife to go to the hardware store and get a roll of duct tape, and if they have chrome plated finish screws, get six. The wife returns with six rolls of duct tape. The husband asks: "Why on earth did you buy six rolls of duct tape?" The wife replied: "You said that if they had chrome screws to get six rolls of tape!"

CAR TALK

The daughter asks her Dad, "Dad, there is something that my boyfriend said to me that I didn't understand. He is so into his cars and said 'that I have a beautiful chassis and lovely dagmars.'" Her Dad said: "You tell your boyfriend that, if he tries to check your oil with his dipstick, I will tighten your lug nuts so hard that his headlights will pop out and he will start leaking oil out of his tailpipe."

(adapted from www.bitoffun.com)

WHO MADE GRANDPOP'S HAIR WHITE?

A teenage boy was teasing his Dad about the strands of white hair mixed in with his black hair: "Dad, why are some of your hairs getting white?" The Dad replied: "Well, son, you are just learning to drive, and every time you rev the engine, chirp the tires, drive too fast, or turn a corner too fast, I get another white hair." The Dad figured he had one-upped his son, when his son replied: "Well Dad, then why are ALL of grandpop's hairs white?"

GET THE QUARTERBACK

A car club member from Iceland named Gudmundur came to the USA for his first visit. Paul and his U.S. hosts wanted to make it a wonderful experience. They picked him up from the airport in a 1937 Chevy street rod and drove him straight to his very first NFL football game. They had great seats right behind the Redskins bench. After the game, Paul asked his Icelandic friend Gudmundur how he liked it. "Oh, I really liked it," he replied, "especially the long passes, interceptions, and vicious tackles. But I just couldn't understand why they were killing each other over 25 cents." Dumbfounded, Paul asked, "What do you mean?" Gudmundur said: "Well, they flipped a coin at the start. One player got it and then for the rest of the game, all the fans kept screaming was 'Get the quarter back! Get the quarter back!' I'm like ...Hellooooo? It's only 25 cents!"

IOWA WINTER

Last winter, Bill and Linda were listening to the Monday morning weather report for Des Moines: "There will be 7 inches of snow today, and you must park your cars on the odd-numbered side of the streets so the snow plow can plow the even side." So Bill parked his '56 Ford Victoria on the odd side on Monday. The next morning, they were listening to the weather report again, which called for 8 more inches, and the radio said that another snow emergency was declared: "You must park your car on the even-numbered side of the streets so the plow can clear the odd side today." So Bill parked his Victoria on the even side on Tuesday. On Friday, the morning weather forecast said, "There will be 9 more inches of snow today, and another snow emergency has been declared. You must park your cars on the ..." ...and the power went out. Bill didn't get the rest of the instructions. He turned to Linda: "What am I going to do now?" Linda replied: "Aw, Bill, just leave the car in the darned garage today."

(adapted from www.mybirdie.ca)

A BOY'S WISH

A Dad was telling his little boy what his own childhood was like. He said, "I had a swing made from a tire; it hung from a tree in our front yard. We drove our old cars to the A&W Root Beer stand and talked about the size of our motors. We'd sneak into drive-in movies in the trunk of the car." The little boy was wide-eyed, taking this in. At last he said, "Gee Dad, I sure wish I'd gotten to know you sooner!"

(adapted from www.beaconseniornews.com)

MONEY WELL-SPENT

After a fender-bender, the teenaged driver called his dad and told him about the damage and said: "Great news, Dad--you haven't been pouring those insurance payments down the drain after all!"

PINK CADILLAC FOR HANUKKAH?

A guy bought his wife a sparkly diamond ring for Hanukkah. Hearing about this generous gift, the guy's friend says: "I thought she wanted a pink Cadillac, right?" The guy says: "Yes, but where am I going to find a fake pink Cadillac?"

FATHERHOOD (TRUE STORY)

My son, Vincent, who drives my old Dodge truck, said: "You're the world's greatest Dad". (Guess I'll let Vince keep my gas credit card for a while.)

APPROPRIATE MEMORIAL?

Bill died, leaving in a will to his wife Edna $30,000 for an elaborate funeral. Bill was a big time classic car collector, but, alas, his wife Edna was not supportive of his expensive hobby. As the last of the visitors departed the services, his wife Edna turned to her dear friend, Sue, and said, "Well, I think Bill would be pleased." "I'm sure you're right," replied Sue, who then lowered her voice and leaned in close. "But how much did this *really* cost?" "All of it," said Edna. "All thirty thousand." Sue, skeptical, said: "I mean, it was nice, but--$30,000?" Edna replied, "Yes. The funeral was $6,500; I donated $500 to the church, and the wake, food and drinks were another $500. I donated $500 to his car club. The rest went for the Memorial Stone." Sue computed quickly and asked, "$22,000 for a Memorial Stone? My goodness, how big is it?" "Two and a half carats," Edna replied smugly.

(adapted from www.estatevaults.com)

SOCCER KIDS

Paul's son Vincent was on a soccer team called the Speedsters. For four weeks in a row, on Wednesday, Paul and Vincent drove to the weekly practice, in his old Ford. But no one else showed—not the coach, not the other kids. Dad Paul told son Vince to text a complaint to the coach. Exasperated, son Vince flipped his hands open in frustration, and said: "He'll just text me the same as the last four weeks." Dad asked: "What did he say." Vince said: "Practice is now on Tuesdays."

VINTAGE 'VETTE FOR $100

Sixteen-year-old Mason drove back to his home in a white 1954 Corvette with a Blue-Flame Six. His mom Michelle said: "Where on earth did you get that?" "From Mrs. Brooks down the street. She only charged me $100—all my dish washing money," he replied with a proud grin. So Mom Michelle marched over to Mrs. Brooks to get the full story. Mrs. Brooks explained that her husband had told her he was going on a business trip to Chicago, but in reality, it turns out he was on a fling with his secretary in Monte Carlo. He called and said he lost all their money gambling and his wallet was stolen and to please sell his precious 1954 'Vette quickly and wire him the money. "So I did," said Mrs. Brooks with a smirk.

CAN'T DRIVE A STICK

A Ford guy shows his friend his fine Customline '56 Ford, and the friend notices that it's a stick shift. The friend says: "I thought that when you bought that car, it had an automatic." The guy says "It did have Fordomatic, but I had it converted to stick shift." "I'll bet that cost a small fortune," says the friend. "Oh, ya. You got that right." "Why would you buy an old car with Fordomatic and then spend all that money to convert it to stick?" The Ford guy says: "My teenage son can't drive a stick."

AT THE USED CAR LOT

Customer to Salesman: "Your big sign says: 'CARS UNDER DEALER COST'. So how can you make a profit?" Salesman: "We make all our profits from repairing them."

DIRECTIONS

Lost Motorist (to Stranger): "How do you get to Tuckahoe from here?" Stranger: "Waaalll, go back about a mile and turn right, but that's left since you haven't turned around yet. Then go apiece for a while, and ask someone else. Come to think of it, you can't get there from here."

STRANDED AT HOME

Teen girl to her boyfriend: "Where is your father?" The kid says: "At home." The girl says: "How do you know?" The kid holds up car keys and says: "Because I have his car."

BACK SEAT DRIVER

A guy was driving his Lincoln and his wife was in the back seat, giving directions every five minutes. It was driving him nuts. The back of his car stalled on the railroad track and she screamed for him to keep going. He looked back and told her: "I've got my end across. So what can you do with your end?"

LADY AT THE BUS STATION

An older woman was on the station platform, pacing impatiently. Another woman walked up to her and asked her: "Are you meeting your husband here." "No," replied the older woman, "I have known him for many years."

FORK IN THE ROAD

Husband: "Uh, oh, we have a flat."

Wife: "I could have told you so. The AAA Trip Tick said there was a fork in the road."

GENEROUS DOBY

To promote his car repair business and help the local car club, Doby raffled off a very small refrigerator, the kind you keep in your garage full of soda or beer. He said its value was $200. Tickets were $1 each. The fellow who won it was overjoyed, put it in his garage, and put a six-pack inside. Next day, the beer was still warm. The winner complained bitterly to Doby. Generous guy that Doby is, he gave him his $1 back.

LIKE FATHER, LIKE SON

The teen son had just successfully changed his first flat tire after getting stranded on the highway. He proudly called his Dad on his cellphone, saying: "What's it like having a talented motor head son?" The Dad replied: "I don't know. Why don't you ask your Grandpa?"

'PEDESTRIAN' DEFINED

"Daddy, in English class today, someone used the word 'pedestrian'. What is a 'pedestrian'?" Dad: "I am a pedestrian. I have a wife, a teenage daughter, and only one car."

KEEP THAT CAR

Steve tried and tried to sell his old car, but had no luck because the car had 250,000 miles on it. He told Annapolis Jack his problem, who advised him: "There is a possibility to make the car easier to sell, but it's not legal." "That doesn't matter if I only can sell the car", says Steve. "Okay," said Jack. Here is the address of a friend of mine. Gary lives across the street from me. Tell him I sent you and he will turn the odometer in your car back to 50,000 miles. Then it will not be a problem to sell your car anymore." Steve made the trip to Gary the mechanic. About one month later, Jack asked: "Did you sell your car?" "Heckfire no," replied Steve. "Why should I? It only has 50,000 miles on it!"

(adapted from www.swapmeetdave.com)

SEVENTEEN ACTUAL STATEMENTS FROM INSURANCE FORMS: DRIVERS DESCRIBED THE ACCIDENT

"1) I pulled away from the side of the road, glanced at my mother-in-law and headed over the embankment.

2) The guy was all over the road. I had to swerve a number of times before I hit him.

3) In an attempt to kill a fly I drove into a telephone pole.

4) I had been driving for forty years when I fell asleep at the wheel and had an accident.

5) I was on the way to the doctor with rear end trouble when my universal joint gave way causing me to have an accident.

6) An invisible car came out of nowhere, struck my car and vanished.

7) The pedestrian had no idea which way to run so I ran over him.

8) Coming home, I drove into the wrong house and collided with a tree I don't have.

9) I thought my window was gone, but I found it was up when I put my head through it."

10) I saw two kangaroos having it off in the middle of the road. So I hit them, which caused me to ejaculate though the sunroof.

11) The accident was caused by me waving to the man I hit last week.

12) No witnesses would admit having seen the mishap until after it happened.

13) I saw a slow-moving, sad-faced old gentleman as he bounced off the roof of my car.

14) I collided with a stationary truck coming the other way.

15) My car was legally parked as it bucked into another vehicle.

16) I was unable to stop in time and my car crashed into the other vehicle. The driver and passengers then left immediately for a vacation with injuries.

17) The gentleman behind me struck me on the backside. He then went to rest in a bush with just his rear end showing."

(adapted from www.swapmeetdave.com; www.ahajokes.com)

WOULDN'T GIVE A DOLLAR FOR IT (True Story)

I prided myself on my collection of 1955-56 Ford parts. My 85-year-old mother from Las Vegas was visiting Maryland one summer and I was eager to show her my full collection of parts removed from a dozen parts cars. I had two garages full of used parts: hoods, fenders, doors, seats, dashboards, stainless trim, tail lights, grilles, bumpers, bumper guards, patch panels, VIN plates, window glass, regulators, and more. Wide-eyed, mom took it all in. She thought about it carefully, and then said resolutely: "I wouldn't give you a DOLLAR for it."

0-200 GIFT

A husband bought his wife a VW bug for her birthday, "I don't like it", she snapped. "I want something that goes 0-200 in three seconds." So he came back the next day with a bathroom scale.

LOCKER ROOM TALK

A bunch of guys were in the locker room of the gym after an exciting pickle ball game. When a cell phone on the bench rang, a guy picked it up, hit the green button, put it on speaker, and began to talk: "Hello?" The woman said: "Hello darling, it is me; I'm in the leather shop and found this beautiful black leather jacket. It's only $2,000. Can I buy it?" The fellow says: "If you like it, you buy it". Then the woman says: "I also stopped by the Cadillac dealership and saw a new model that has a black leather interior which will match the coat." The fellow says: "Buy it! You will look great in it!" She coos: "Thank you, lovely dovey, see you at home." The fellow hung up. The other guys in the locker room were gaping with amazement at his generosity. Then he asked them: "Does anyone know whose phone this is?"

PAYBACK

Junior had just turned 16 and received his first driver's license. He and Dad went out to the garage and climbed into the old Parklane wagon Ford. Dad immediately headed for the back seat, directly behind Junior. "I'll bet you're back there to get a change of scenery after all those months of sitting in the front passenger seat teaching me how to drive," says Junior to Dad. "Nope," says Dad. "I'm gonna sit here in the back seat and kick the back of your seat as you drive, just like you've been doing to me all these years."

(adapted from www.ajokeaday.com)

NICE BOYFRIEND?

A teenaged girl brought her new boyfriend home to meet her parents. They're appalled by his 60's haircut and old rat rod Chevy truck. Later, the girl's Mom says, "Dear, he doesn't seem to be a very nice boy." "Oh, please Mom!" says the daughter. "If he wasn't nice, would he be picking up trash on the side of the road for 500 hours of community service?"

AUTOBIOGRAPHY

Q: Why did the girl ask her parents about all the cars they had ever owned?

A: She was writing an auto-biography.

VERY ORIGINAL DATE

Q: How was your blind date?

A: Terrible, He showed up in a 1929 Ford.

Q: What's so terrible about that?

A: He was the original owner!

MISSED THE POINT

A husband and wife went to a counselor after 15 years of marriage. The counselor asked them what the problem was, and the wife went into a tirade listing every problem they have ever had in the 15 years they've been married: "He's always in the garage working on his Mustang with the 351 Cleveland engine. He's always going to car shows. He spends way too much money on chrome car parts." She went on and on. Finally, the counselor got up, walked around the desk, embraced the wife, and kissed her passionately. The woman shut up and sat quietly in a daze. The counselor turned to the husband and said: "This is what your wife needs at least three times a week. Can you make this happen?" The husband thought for a moment and replied "Well, I can drop her off here on Mondays, Wednesdays, and Fridays. But on Tuesday I go to my car club meetings, on Thursdays I work on my car. On Fridays I go to a local cruise-in at McDonalds and on Saturdays and Sundays I go to the big shows with trophies and dash plaques. So yes, I am proud to say I can handle it."

(adapted from www.urbanflyfisher.com)

BE HONEST WITH YOUR WIFE

Be honest with your wife about how much you paid for each classic car. If you die, your wife will sell your classic car for the price you told her you paid for it.

CHAPTER FOURTEEN

CRUISERS AT CAR SHOWS, SWAP MEETS, AND THE RACES

Cruisers (euphuism for aficionados) go to car club conventions, take tour buses, write ads on dating sites, attend swap meets, visit car auctions, and cheer at race tracks and drag strips. In this book, as they do so, we will chuckle at their absurd adventures.

FLYING TO THE TWIN CITIES CAR CONVENTION? CONSIDER "OLI AIR"

(You must read this aloud with the proper Scandinavian-almost-Canadian accent!)

"Ya' shure, ya' betcha! Dis is da' latest air service to sprout up in Minnysota [Also serving Visconsin, Nort and Sout Dakota and Montana]. If you are travelin' soon, consider Oli Air, da' nofrills airline where flyin' is an upliftin' experience. Everyone is first class on any Oli Air flight. Meals are potluck. Rows 1-6, bring rolls; 7-15, bring a salad; 16-21, a main dish, and 22-30, a dessert. Lunch is buffet style with da' coffee pot up front. Basses and tenors please sit in da' rear of de' aircraft, it sounds better when da' signin' starts. Hymnals are in da' seat pocket in front of you. All fares are by freewill offering and da' plane will not land 'til da' budget is met. In de' event of a sudden loss of cabin pressure, de' are frankly gonna to be real surprised and so will Captain Olson, because de' fly right around is two tousan feet, so loss of cabin pressure would probably indicate da' Second Coming. If da' masks fall out, it is probably because of turbulence, so please stuff 'dem back into place. De' use of cell phones on da' plane is OK because dere is not much of a plane's seat-of-da-pants navigational system to interfere wit. Da' stewardesses are corn-fed farm girls and will lead us in dis prayer: 'Fadar, Son, and Holy Ghost, may we land softly in St. Paul, or pretty close.' Amen."

(adapted from www.hotrodders.com and www.audiokarma.org)

SWEET BECKY

Car clubs have all sorts of characters with wonderful and terrible personalities. Sweet Becky was a person who could always find something nice to say about someone, no matter how terrible and despicable they happened to be. Owen was one such despicable person. He cheated by voting for his own car (against the rules). He smudged the other cars with grease when the owners weren't looking. He "put the make" on other guys' wives. He was foul-mouthed. A friend came up with challenge for Becky. "Becky, I'll bet you $1 that you can't find one good thing to say about Owen." Becky thought and thought, agreed to the bet, and said: "Owen has a really nice wife...", as she took her friend's dollar.

BRITISH BUS RIDE

A group of good ol' boy car guy tourists visit London. They charter a bus to go to Buckingham Palace, and for some reason all are seated on the upper level. The tour leader, sitting on the bottom, goes up the steps to the top level to see how they're doing. He finds them all sitting tight-lipped, eyes wide open and with terrified looks on their faces. Their hands are gripping the seatbacks with white knuckles. "What's wrong with you guys?" the tour leader asks. "This is great scenery. Everybody downstairs is enjoying the ride!" "Sure," said a guy in front. "That's because you have a driver!"

CLUMSY

Lady heard talking to her friend at a car show criticizing her husband: "My husband is so clumsy with car tools that they have a special ambulance on call, reserved just for him, and a bed with his name at the hospital."

I'M SURE

At a car show, a guy falls to the ground, and he does not seem to be breathing. His buddy calls 911 and says: "I think my friend is dead. What do I do?" The emergency operator tells him to calm down, saying: "Let's make sure he's dead first." She hears a clank from a tire iron. Then she hears: "OK, I'm sure. Now what?"

JUST LIKE YOU?

Car club President Doby said to a member. "Thank you, Spencer, for your membership. I wish I had exactly five members like you." "Gosh, it's nice to hear that, but I'm kind of surprised," admitted Spencer. "You know that I argue about the judging, that dues are too high, and why rice rockets are allowed in the club." The President said, "I'd still like five members like you. The problem is, I have twenty!"

FOUL PLAY

A guy drove his old Ford to a car show, the kind with open hoods, and noticed lots of birds flying around his engine compartment. After the show, it would not start. He suspected fowl play.

THE REALLY STUPID TERRORIST

Did you hear about the very dumb terrorist who tried to blow up his car at a car show? He burned his lips on his tailpipe!

FORTIFIED

A church, Our Lady of 59th Street, sponsored a '50's sock hop and had invited owners of old cars to come to help set the tone. The priest approached the owner of a 1949 Hudson and asked: "Are you prepared for this, with wild teens running around and crazy dancing and all?" "I think so," the man replied. The priest responded. "I mean, are you prepared spiritually?" "Oh sure," came the reply. "I've got a six-pack under the seat. Want one?"

GREAT RECEPTION

Two antennae met at a car show and decided to get married. The wedding was nice but the reception was terrific.

ON A SENIOR DATING SITE

"Dear Ladies: I've sure gotten old! I've had two by-pass surgeries, a hip replacement, new knees, fought prostate cancer and diabetes, I'm half blind, can't hear anything quieter than a jet engine, take 40 different medications that make me dizzy, winded, and subject to blackouts. Have lost most of my teeth and my friends. But thank God, I still have my driver's license. So if you are up for a wild ride with a big guy in a little sports car, call me." Signed, Rich.

(adapted from www.celticradio.net)

SUNDAY CAR SHOW

By the time my friend Russell arrived to the Sunday car show it was half over. "Why are you so late?" I asked. Russell explained, "I had to toss a coin to decide between going to church and coming here." "How long could that have taken you?", I said. "Well," said Russell, "I had to toss it 14 times!"

(adapted from www.ditching9to5.com)

UH OH...

A national car club which had large, out-of-town shows to its national and regional meets decided to give free registrations to wives who were registered as accompanying their husbands on car club conventions. They had expected gracious "thank you" letters from the wives when they asked them how they enjoyed specific convention events. Letters from the wives came pouring in, asking "What trip?"

SEE WHAT HAPPENS...

A ragged smelly bum asked a man on the street for two dollars. "Will you use it to pay for admissions to car shows?", the man asks, to which the bum replies, "No." "Will you buy old car parts with it?" Once again the bum replies, "No." "Will you come home with me so my wife can see what happens to a man who doesn't spend money on car shows and parts?"

FIVE SLOGANS ON T-SHIRTS AT CAR SHOWS

1. I don't suffer from insanity, I enjoy every minute of it.

2. You're just jealous because the voices only talk to me.

3. Beauty is in the eye of the beer holder.

4. Consciousness: that annoying time between naps.

5. Wrinkled: Not one of the things I wanted to be when I grew up.

SPI-DER! SPI-DER! SPI-DER!

A guy at a car show has a little pet spider on his shoulder. He says, "This spider is stronger than any of you!! Watch!" He sets the spider on the ground and the spider easily picks up a can of car wax. "That's nothing!!" shouts a guy, "Make him pick up something heavy!" The spider then picked up a floor jack. Then the guy wants to really impress his friends, so the guy says; "Now my spider will pick up the truck with every one of us on it!!" Twenty guys climb on the back of the truck cheering "Spi-der, spi-der, spi-der…" Suddenly, a woman walks up; and sees 20 men on the truck. She walks boldly over to the spider, steps on him and squishes him back and forth, and taunts the guys, and says, "You bunch of sissies, scared of a little spider!!"

WHICH IS WHICH?

A not-too-smart barber Ken (nicknamed "Scissorhands") had a 1956 Crown Vic and his friend had one too. At car shows he always had trouble figuring out which was which. A friend suggested that Ken really detail out his car so it would be so much cleaner than his friend's car. That worked fine until the other guy detailed out his car too. Finally, a friend suggested checking the tire size, suspecting that one car ran 6:70/15 and the other ran 7:10/15. That worked, because, sure enough, the Ken's black car ran 6:70/15's and his friend's white car ran 7:15/15's.

T-BUCKET HAIRCUT

The morning of the big parade, a man and a little boy entered a barber shop together. "Give me the full treatment," the man said. "I want to look good in my old T-Bucket hot rod in the parade!" After the man received a shave, manicure, and haircut, he placed the boy in the chair. "I'm going to buy a new tie to wear for the parade," he said. "I'll be back in a few minutes." When the boy's haircut was done and the man still hadn't returned, the barber said, "It looks like your daddy forgot all about you." "That wasn't my daddy," said the boy. "He just walked up, took me by the hand and said, "Come on little guy, we're both gonna get a free haircut!"

(adapted from www.wnd.com)

FAIR JUDGEMENT

Cars in a show were being judged on a 100 point scale. A guy who wanted to win decided to cheat, and secretly slipped the judge an envelope. Inside was a note which said "Car #57 - $1 per point" along with a $100 bill. The guy did not win a trophy. Afterwards he walked up to the judge, who gave him back his envelope with only $50 in it...and this note: "It was only a 50 point car."

THE PRICE OF ADMISSION

A fellow came upon a car show at a mall, and walked along a row of colorful 50's cars. He asked an owner: "Is there a price of admission?" The owner replied: "No admission price, as long as I don't have to listen to you talk about the fact that you once had a car like this, and you got your first kiss at the drive-in, and you sold it too cheap, yadda, yadda..."

HIS LOVE IS TRUE (EMAIL)

Subject: I Love You Still

Dearest Lauren,

I'm so sorry for the things I said. I've been unable to sleep since I broke off our relationship last month. I think about you day and night. Your absence is breaking my heart and recently I've begun to realize that nobody can take your place. Sweetheart, I miss you so much. Please call me.

All my love, Robert

P.S. Congratulations on winning that new Dodge Viper from the Dodge Dealership.

CAR SHOW BRAGGER

"I brought a '69 Mustang to the show." "Really? I have six old cars." "Wow, what are they?" "I've got a 1941 Ford with a 429 Cobra Jet Engine, a 1949 Hudson done as a rat rod, a 1937 Chevy humpback sedan, a pink and white 1955 Ford Crown Victoria, a 1955 Crown Victoria Glasstop, a 1955 Ford Sunliner convertible, and a 1966 Thunderbird convertible." "Wow, with so many, how do you decide which car to bring to a show?" "Whichever will start."

"So what did you drive to the car show today?" "Err...none of them...I took a taxi."

BOB THE VENDOR

Bob was an experienced old car parts vendor, and he hated it when someone got the best of him in a deal. At an indoor parts meet, Bob had a pair of large 12 volt horns priced at $5. Paul ambled up, and asked Bob if the horns worked. "Sure", Bob said, as he pulled out a 12 volt battery. "BEEP!" went the horns, which jolted everyone within 100 feet. Paul handed Bob the $5, and Bob handed over the horn. A fellow who was 100 feet away heard the horns blow, and walked over to Paul, holding the horns. "How much for the horns?" he asked Paul. (At this point, Bob was still holding the $5 bill which Paul had given him for the horns). Paul said $30, and the guy immediately gave Paul $30 for the horns. All this occurred as Bob stood there, jaw dropped open, holding Paul's $5 bill. (*P.S. True story. It happened to me and Bob!*)

DEAD WEIGHT KEVIN

Doby met Bob at the car club meeting one day and said, "I understand you experienced a great tragedy last week." Bob nodded, his eyes growing dark with the memory. "I was at Carlisle Flea Market with Kevin," he said, "and the poor fellow had a heart attack halfway through." Doby said, "I understand you carried him back to the truck. That must have been difficult, considering that Kevin weighs two hundred fifty pounds." Bob said, "Oh, it wasn't the carrying that was so hard. It was putting him down at every vendor, and then picking him up again. All 500 spaces!"

TO TELL THE TRUTH

A clergyman was at the Carlisle swap meet and came upon three guys having a very lively discussion. "What's going on?" he asked. "We all found this brand new Snap-On screwdriver set on the ground at exactly the same moment, so we decided that whichever one of us can tell the biggest lie will get to keep the screwdrivers." The reverend was taken aback. "You men shouldn't be having a contest telling lies!" he exclaimed. He then launched into a ten-minute sermon against lying, beginning, "Don't you men know it's a sin to lie," and ending with,

"I never told a lie. Never!" There was a silence, and just as the clergyman was beginning to think he'd gotten through to them, one guy gave a deep sigh and said, "All right, give the reverend the screwdrivers."

(adapted from www.aish.com)

THE VALUE OF DREW

A group of friends went to Carlisle for parts and paired off in twos for the day. Late that afternoon one of the guys returned alone, staggering under the weight of a '56 Ford hood. "Where's Drew?", the others asked. "Drew had a stroke. He's a couple of miles back". "You left Drew layin' out there and carried the hood back?", they inquired. "This is a rust-free hood...some Ford guy might steal it, but I figured no one's gonna steal Drew!"

TWO FINAL REQUESTS

Bay City Bob decided to prepare his will and told his lawyer that he had two final requests. First, he wanted to be cremated. Second, he wanted his ashes scattered over Carlisle Fairgrounds. He wanted his friends to visit him spring, summer, fall, and All Fords weekends.

GOOD DEALS?

After Carlisle had concluded, three car dealers were discussing the results with one another. The first dealer said, "The car corral worked out great for us! We bought four used cars." The second dealer said, "We did even better...we bought six used cars." Skip, the third dealer said, "We did even better...we got rid of our ten worst cars."

CARLISLE RUDENESS

At Carlisle very early one morning, the Diamond Back Classics sign read: "CLEARANCE. WIDE WHITE RADIALS, ALL SIZES, FIVE FOR $100." A very long line formed in back of the truck, anticipating the start of the sale. A man named Buddy pushed his way to the front of the line, only to be pushed back amid loud and colorful curses. On Buddy's second attempt, he was punched square in the jaw and knocked around a bit, then thrown to the end of the line again. As Buddy got up the second time, he said to the person at the end of the line: "That does it! If they hit me one more time, I won't open the truck!"

(adapted from www.khairul-today.blogspot.com)

GOOD IDEA FOR CHARITY

A guy was buying re-plated '55 Merc tail lights for his 1955 Ford Sunliner for $1,300. The seller said to the buyer: "You know, you really should take your $1,300 and give it to charity." The buyer said: "OK, good idea. I'll buy the taillights, but you have to give *your* $1,300 to charity."

SOMETHING VERY CHEAP

At a swap meet, a guy was looking over some vintage tires for his 1963 Galaxie XL. The vendor said: "How about these wide white radials for $250 each?" "No, I want something cheaper," said the guy. "How about these wide white bias ply tires for $125 each?", said the vendor. "No, that's still too much money," said the guy, "Show me something cheaper." "How about these used bias ply wide whites for $40 each?" said the vendor. "No, that's still too much," said the guy, "show me something really cheap." So the vendor handed the guy a mirror.

CARLISLE...THURSDAY VS. SUNDAY

A preacher and his parishioner, both classic car enthusiasts, argued about the merits of going to All-Chrysler Carlisle on Thursday vs. Sunday. The preacher liked to go on Thursday to get first crack at the goods. The parishioner liked to go on Sunday and skip church when the stuff that did not sell earlier would be marked down. The preacher pronounced: "The so-called good things that come to those who wait will be the leftover things left behind by those who got there first."

THE REASON

At the Carlisle swap meet, a policeman went up to a vendor named Drew selling car parts and said, "I'm sorry, you can't sell that stuff without a license." The vendor replied, "I knew I wasn't selling any, but I didn't know the reason."

AUCTION ACTION (TRUE STORY)

Paul went with his friend Skip to a "dealers only" auction of collector cars and motorcycles in Bel Aire, MD. It is the annual auction of collector-type vehicles (not garden-variety used cars). Skip told Paul: "Just bring your cash, and if your bid wins the car, we will use my dealer license to finish the transaction." There were hundreds of dealers bidding, while Skip and Paul stood in the very back on a wooden bench. Paul had his life savings, $4,400, with him. A Ninja-type motorcycle came up for bids, but Paul had no interest. The bidding quickly advanced to $4,000. At that instant, a very striking woman with long blonde hair entered by the auctioneer. She was wearing skin-right black leathers with tassels and nickel studs up and down her outfit. Huge hoop earrings and viper red lipstick completed her ensemble. Paul nudged Skip, and pointed at her, and asked Skip, "Who is that?" Just then the auctioneer pointed right at Paul and the auctioneer said: "$4,100." Skip said: "I don't know, but you just bid $4,100 on that motorcycle." Fortunately, another bidder quickly shouted $4,200, and Paul kept his hands tucked deep in his pockets for the rest of the auction.

FRAMED

Q. Is it true that Fireball Roberts was arrested for stealing his own self-portrait from the Indy 500 Hall of Fame?

A. No, it's not true. He was framed!

FAIR COMPENSATION

Legendary African-American race car driver, Wendell Scott (1921-1990), is rumored to have been cutting the grass at his fine home in the Deep South. A neighbor who did not know him pulled up to the sidewalk and asked: "My good man, how much do you charge the lady of the house to mow a yard of that size?" The race car driver politely replied: "She does not pay me anything ma'am, but she does let me sleep with her every night."

DRAG STRIP

Tommy: "I'm upset what the county did to the local dragstrip. They tore up the asphalt, did away with the parking area, removed the stands, and got rid of the snack bar." Paul: "Terrible. Sounds like they've got a lot on their hands." *(Get it? A "lot")*.

50 BUCKS IS 50 BUCKS

Ken and his wife Edna went to stock car races every month. Ken would say: "Edna, I'd like to pay that driver to take me for a ride in that race car." Edna always replied, "I know, Ken, but that race car has no glass in the windows. You could fly out. PLUS, that race car ride is fifty bucks, and fifty bucks is fifty bucks." Finally, Ken and Edna went to the races, and Ken said," Edna, I'm 75 years old. If I don't ride that race car now, I might never get another chance." To this, Edna replied, "Ken, that race car ride is fifty bucks, and fifty bucks is fifty bucks." The race car driver overheard the old couple and said, "Folks, I'll make you a deal. I'll take the BOTH of you for a race car ride. If you can BOTH stay quiet for the entire ride and don't say a word or scream and holler, I won't charge you a penny. But if you say one word its fifty dollars." Ken and Edna agreed and into the race car they climbed. The race car driver did all kinds of fancy maneuvers, donuts, spins, and jumped ditches to cause big bumps, but not a word was heard. When they finally stopped, the race car driver turned to Ken and said, "By golly, I did everything I could to get you to yell out, but you didn't. I'm impressed!" Ken replied, "Well to tell you the truth, I almost said something when Edna fell out the back window, but you know, fifty bucks is fifty bucks!"

(adapted from www.fellowshipoftheminds.com)

NO BALANCE

I was planning to buy a vintage Chevy Impala at a large regional auction and was not sure how much was in my checking account. I walked up to the lady teller at my bank and asked her to check my balance. She immediately leaned over the counter and pushed me!

SEEING EYE DOG

A blind man took his dog to a car show. All of a sudden he starts swinging his Seeing Eye dog in circles over his head by the dog's leash. A car guy runs up to him and says: "Mister, what are you doing?" The blind man says: "Just looking around at the cars!"

CHAPTER FIFTEEN

CRUISERS JUST CRUISIN'

As we cruise out and around, life happens. Funny, outlandish events occur with genies (do they exist?), talking parrots, weirdos, gearheads, naïve Minnesota farmers, Russians, crows, old biddy ladies, Army generals, squirrels, hitchhikers, alligators, farmers, God impersonators, bus drivers, frogs, and goats. How can these kinds of encounters NOT be comical?

THE PROPER BOSTONIAN

Cleveland Amory wrote a book with the above title. In the book, he tells about the wealthy proper Bostonian lady who decided to commit suicide. She had her chauffer drive her off a cliff!

SKIP AND CHIP

Skip and Chip cruise to an evening car show in Skip's vintage Pontiac convertible. Chip says to Skip: "Look up and tell me what you see". Skip says: "I see millions of stars", Chip says: "What else do you see?" Skip says: "The cosmos is huge. I see millions of galaxies with billions of planets. And theologically, I see that God is all powerful and we are insignificant specks." Chip says with exasperation: "Skip, you bonehead, you missed the point. There is a huge hole in your convertible top!"

SON BUGS DAD

Dad takes his six-year-old son proudly cruising in his classic car to the A & W Root Beer Drive In. They ordered dinner and the curb girl hung a tray on their window with their food. "Dad", the boy asked, "are bugs good to eat?" The Dad said: "That's a disgusting thing to talk about so, later..." After dinner, Dad asked his son: "So son, what was the question you wanted to ask about?" "Oh, never mind, Dad, there was a bug in your root beer, but he's dead now."

NO BIZ...

A guy is just outside a Jiffy Lube wearing gorilla suit, holding a sign that says: "OIL CHANGE $19.95 WHILE YOU WAIT." A fellow cruising by stops and walks up to him and says: "Hey buddy, why don't you get a *real* job?" The guy in the gorilla suit replies: "What, and get out of show business?"

GENIE GRANTS THREE WISHES

Three people ----an editor, a photographer, and a news reporter are covering a county commissioners meeting in Centreville. They decide to walk in the sand by the Chesapeake Bay. Halfway up the beach, they stumbled upon a lamp and cleaned it. A genie comes out of the lamp. Seeing three people, he offers each one a wish in thanks for them releasing him from the lamp. Doug, the photographer, went first. "I would like to be photographing custom car shows in sunny California." The genie agreed to Doug's wish and "poof", he was off to Los Angeles. Kristian, the journalist, was next. "I would like to be interviewing exciting NASCAR drivers at Daytona and Indianapolis and such." The genie granted her wish and "poof", sent her off to the races. Last, but not least, it was Angela the editor's turn. "And what would your wish be?" asked the genie. "I want them both back after lunch today", replied the editor, "The deadline for Wednesday's newspaper is in about ten hours.

POINT OF VIEW

When a visitor to a small town in Georgia came upon a young carjacker attacking an old lady, he quickly grabbed the criminal and throttled him with his two hands. A reporter saw this occur, he shook the hand of the visitor and told him his valiant feat would be in the paper next day, as: "Valiant Local Man Saves Woman by Throttling Carjacker." The hero told the journalist that he wasn't from that town. "Well, then," the reporter said, "The headline will say, 'Georgia Man Saves Old Woman by Throttling Carjacker'." "Actually," the man said, "I'm from Connecticut." "You are a Yankee?" asked the reporter. "In that case," the reporter said in a huff, "the headline should read, 'Yankee Injures Local Teen'."

INDIAN PREDICTIONS

A film crew was on location deep in the Arizona desert. One day an old Indian drove up to the film site in a 1958 Pontiac Chiefton. He went up to the director and said, "Tomorrow rain." The next day it rained. Two days later, the Indian walked over to the director and said, "Tomorrow will storm." And the next day a hailstorm occurred. "This Indian is wonderful," said the director. He told his assistant to hire the Indian to predict the weather. After a few more correct predictions, the director was worried since he needed a sunny day for tomorrow's shoot. He needed the Indian's prediction. The Indian shrugged his shoulders. "Don't know," he said. "Car radio broken."

(suggested by www.jokeindex.com)

VERY TIRED

Q. Did you hear about the good ol' boy who had been run over by a monster truck with huge tires?

A. When Doug from the local paper spoke with him in the hospital, he was conscious but said that he was overly tired.

(www.upjoke.com)

ONE FOR THE MONEY...

Doug, a nosey news reporter, was interviewing Carol, an 80-year old woman who had just gotten married for the fourth time in her life.

The interviewer was asking her questions about her life, about how it felt to be marrying again at 80, and about her four spouses.

The reporter asks her if she wouldn't mind telling him a little bit about her four husbands. The first, she says, was a wealthy medical doctor who drove a Rolls Royce. The second was a well-healed car collector who loved going to car shows.

The third fellow ran the Christmas tree lights at drag races. And the fourth ran his streamliner to 400 miles per hour on the salt flats. The reporter asks her why, if there was any reason, she chose to marry those specific people. She responds, "Well, I married one for the money, two for the show. Three to get ready, and four to go!"

CURSED HORSE

A fellow was enjoying a drive through the country in his old car, when it coughed, sputtered, backfired, and died. He decided to finish his trip on horseback, and walked to the nearest stable to rent a horse. The stable owner had just one horse to rent, and explained that his former owner was very religious. The owner explained that when you want him to bolt forward, shout "Holy Moly!" And when you want him to stop, "Lord Almighty, Stop!" The fellow agreed, and shouted "Holy Moly!", and the nag took off with a bolt, racing to a mountain top. "Whoa, hold up, you dumb nag," but the horse kept running to a steep ledge. Then he remembered, and screamed "Lord Almighty, stop!" in the horse's ear, and the horse stopped abruptly. He then leaned over the horse's neck to see a 500 foot drop to a raging river below. Terrified, he cried out: "Holy Moly!"

DRIVE RIGHT IN

A fellow was struggling to get his car out of a shallow pond, and a local farmer asked: "How did you come to drive into the pond, my young man?" The young man replied: "I did not come to drive in to the pond, I came to park next to it and go fishing."

STRONGEST GUY

A guy walks into a busy gym and asks in a loud manly voice: "Who is the strongest guy in here?" Two big guys named Vince and Ben shout out simultaneously: "I am!" "Great," says the guy, "Will you please help me push my car to the gas station?"

TALKING PARROT

A burglar broke into a garage, intent on stealing a vintage Chevy Impala wlth a 348 V-8. He was nervous, but then heard a voice say: "Jesus is watching your every move." The burglar turned his flashlight in the direction of the voice, and saw a green parrot in a cage. "Was that you talking?", he said to the parrot. The parrot said: "Yes, it was me, Moses." He asked the parrot what kind of guy would name a parrot "Moses?" The parrot replied: "The same kind of guy just outside who carries a .357 magnum and named his pit bull "Jesus."

VAN AT THE RACES

"Knock-Knock. Who's there?" "Van Gogh." "Van Gogh who?" "Ready—set—Van Gogh!"

CAR IN A DITCH

"Knock-Knock." "Who's there?" "Carina." "Carina who?" "Carina ditch. Can I use your phone?"

COMING OR GOING?

"Knock-Knock." "Who's there?" "Car man or Motor man." "Car man or Motor man who?" "You don't know whether you're a Car man or a Motor man?"

DATA

"Knock-Knock." "Who's there?" "Data." "Data who?" "Data new hairdo or did you just walk through a car wash?"

AVIS

"Knock-Knock." "Who's there?" "Avis." "Avis who?" "Avis just passing by and noticed your old car in the driveway."

BLISTERS FROM BROOM

Wife: "I have blisters on my hands from the broom."

Husband: (Cynically) "Next time, take the car."

ONE SHORT

Too many teenagers piled into a small car. The driver called out, "Anyone here know how to pray?" One kid said: "I do." "Good," said the driver. "You pray. The rest of us will put on seat belts. We're one belt short."

LONG BUS TRIP

On a long Trailways Bus trip across the country, a young woman finally said to the driver: "Aren't we ever going to get to Los Angeles? Can't you see I'm well along in pregnancy? Are you going to help me deliver this baby if we don't get there in time?" The driver said: "Madam, you should *not* have gotten on my bus in this condition?" The lady replied: "I didn't."

NUDIST CRASH

A guy crashed into the fence of a nudist camp. Someone came running out and said, "Why didn't you look where you were going?" He said, "I couldn't. I was too busy going where I was looking!"

THE MONK AND THE YANKEE

An English monk came upon an American at the side of the road, trying to fix a Jaguar in the dark. He offered to help. The Yankee was frustrated with Lucas British electronics. *(There are many American jokes about "Lucas, Price of Darkness".)* He said sarcastically to the monk in a sneering way: "Are you Lucas, Prince of Darkness?" The monk did not enjoy the Yankee's humor one bit. He pointed at the Yankee with his cane and said: "There is an idiot at the end of this cane." To which the Yankee replied: "Yes, but at which end?"

(So much for British-American relations.)

THAT'S LIVING

A well-regarded member of a large car club died, and after the black hearse followed a 1957 Cadillac, a 1955 Crown Victoria, a 1954 Corvette, and other beautiful classics. "Wow," said one onlooker to another watching the procession. "Now that's what I call living."

GONE NUCLEAR

Did you hear about the atomic scientist who decided to go on fishing on his vacation? Before he took his Jeep into the country, he hung up a sign on his office door: GONE FISSION!

LIGHTS ON OR OFF?

If you like Pope Francis I, drive with your lights ON Friday night. If you like Kim Jong Un, dictator of North Korea, drive with your lights OFF Friday night.

FLYING VS. DRIVING

Scott and Robb were arguing, flying is safer than driving, driving is safer than flying. "Listen, why don't you take a philosophic approach? Tell yourself that if your number isn't up, then it isn't up, and take the plane" said Scott. Said Robb: "And what difference would it make if *my* number wasn't up, if the *pilot's* number is up?"

LATE

A gas jockey, who commuted from home, arrived late to his gas station said to his boss: "Sorry I'm late. I got stuck behind a slowpoke doing the speed limit."

A RAISE?

I told my boss that three companies were after me and I need a raise. My boss asked, "What companies?" I replied: "The Nation's Bank for my car payment, Western Auto for my new tires, and State Farm for my car insurance."

HOMER AND JETHRO

Homer and Jethro drove by a gas station. Homer says, "These prices are awful. They just keep going higher!" Jethro replies, "It doesn't affect me at all. I always put in just $20 worth."

GOOD ADVICE

A man approached a local person in a town he was visiting. He asked the local: "What's the quickest way to Des Moines, Iowa? I'm going to the car club convention there." The local scratched his head. "Are you walking or driving?" he asked the stranger. "I'm driving." The local replied: "THAT'S the quickest way!"

MINNESOTA VS. IOWA: FOUR QUESTIONS

There is a battle of wits between Minnesota and Iowa residents.

Question 1: "What do they call reruns of Hee Haw in Minnesota?"

Answer 1: "A documentary!"

Question 2: "Did you hear about the $3 million dollar Minnesota lottery?"

Answer 2: "The winner gets $3 per year for a million years!"

Question 3: "How can you tell if an Iowa farmer is married?"

Answer 3: "There's dried chewing tobacco on BOTH sides of his truck!"

Question 4: "How many Iowans does it take to eat a possum?"

Answer 4: "Two. One to eat and one to watch out for traffic and catch more!"

WOMEN AND MEN: 3,000 MILE ROUTINE OIL CHANGE

WOMEN

"1. Pull up to Jiffy Lube when the mileage reaches 3,000 since the last oil change.

2. Drink a cup of coffee.

3. Fifteen minutes later, write a $30 check

4. With clean hands and clothes, drive away with a properly-maintained vehicle and a reminder sticker on the windshield for the next change.

MEN

1. Friday, go to Autozone parts store and write a $125 check for 12 quarts of oil, new filter, kitty litter, hand cleaner, rags, the latest design of oil filter wrench, rubber gloves, and why not--a new creeper and set of jack stands.

2. Saturday morning, put on overalls; clean out garage so the car can be driven at least halfway in by noon.

3. Discover that the used oil container is full. Drive to recycling center to dispose of old oil.

4. Return in time for 1 p.m. lunch. First beer 2 p.m., put on some 60's music to get in the mood.

5. Pump up hydraulic jack, unbox new jack stands with glee, feel remorse because they are made by someone who does not speak your language.

6. Look for 9/16 box end wrench. Give up search, use vice grips.

7. Unscrew drain plug, oil runs down your glove, up your sleeve. Drop drain plug in oil pan.

8. Clean up, have another beer at 3 p.m., figure out why new oil filter wrench slips.

9. Buddy shows up; discusses old cars, tells you his favorite jokes from Paul Placek's new book "1,000 Jokes For Auto Aficionados". Both laugh hilariously.

10. Throw kitty litter on oil spilled on garage floor.

11. Screw in new oil filter, pull drain pan from under car, roll out from under.

12. Remove jack stands and jack while humming "Little Deuce Coupe" and downing a third beer.

13. Add five cans of fresh oil to motor, check for leaks underneath. Whoops! Five quarts on the floor. Forgot about drain plug! Use up all kitty litter plus Miss January through Miss December 1992. Retrieve drain plug from used oil pan, jack up car, screw in drain plug, un-jack car, feeling grateful that at least you did not start the engine without oil.

14. Add five more quarts of oil, smug that at least you had the forethought to buy a dozen.

15. The fourth beer is to celebrate a job well done, and it's 5 p.m., dinner time.

16. Forget to note when oil change was done, and drive car for 7,000 miles, now two quarts low.

17. Six months later, repeat steps 1-16 as necessary."

(www.wranglerforum.com)

PERK THE COOK

At my family's A & W Root Beer Drive-In Restaurant in Sanford, Florida, we had a cook named Perk. She was a large lady with a good sense of humor. One of our curb girls took an order for a Papa Burger done medium well with lettuce, tomatoes, cheese, onions, ketchup, mustard, and mayo. When the curb girl delivered it to his car, the customer took a great big bite out of it. He called the curb girl back, insisting he wanted well done, and *no* ketchup, mustard, or mayo. He sent it back to the cook. Perk the cook remade the burger exactly how the customer wanted it. Then Perk took a great big bite out of it! And the curb girl took it back to the customer in the car with Perk's big bite taken out of it. And he ate it! *(True story by Paul Placek).*

DRIVER'S TEST RESULTS

Last night my son came home from a date and said, "I have good news and bad news. The good news is that I got 18 out of 20 on my driver's test." I said, "Great! Now what's the bad news?" He said, "They were all pedestrians."

TRANSLATED...

What a man says to his wife or girlfriend (and what it really means). "Let's take your car" really means..."Mine is full of beer cans, burger wrappers, and completely out of gas."

(www.gameboomers.com)

NEXT OF KIN

A car was involved in a horrific accident in front of Madison Square Garden in New York City. As expected, a large crowd gathered around the accident scene. Just then, an overzealous newspaper reporter named Christine, anxious to get the story, arrived on the scene. However, she could not get near the car. Being a clever sort, Christine started shouting loudly, "Let me through! Let me through! I am the daughter of the victim!" The crowd made way for the reporter. Lying in front of the car was a horse (which had pulled a carriage through Central Park).

IT WAS TRUE!

In Ocean Springs, Mississippi, there is a sign that reads: "Speed limit 25 mph unless otherwise posted." Right below it is another sign that reads: "Speed limit 30 mph."

TIME FOR A PILL

On a bus trip, the little old lady seated herself right behind the bus driver. Every ten minutes or so she'd pipe up, "Have we reached Minnehaha Falls yet, sonny?" "No, Ma'am, not yet. I'll let you know," the bus driver replied, after she asked him three times. At last the little town came into view. With exasperation the bus driver slammed on the airbrakes, pulled over and announced: "This is where you get out, lady." "Is this Minihaha Falls?" "YES!", he bellowed, "You may get out!" "Oh, I'm going all the way to St. Paul, sonny," she explained sweetly. "It's just that my daughter told me that when we got this far, I should take my vitamins."

(adapted from www.lolwithgod.com)

16-YEAR-OLD GEARHEAD?

A girl got a car with an automatic transmission for her 16th birthday. The car works fine during the day, but at night, she complained, it goes nowhere! In a huff she called the dealer to explain the problem. The dealer said: "Get over here immediately, Ma'am." The dealer says to the 16-year-old: "I can't find any problems with the car. Are you sure you are using the right gears?" She says: "How on earth could you ask such a question? I'm not stupid you know. Of course I am using the right gears; I use 'D' during the day and 'N' at night."

TAKEN CAB

I would like to share a personal experience with my friends about drinking and driving. Two days ago I was out for an evening with friends and had several cocktails followed by some rather nice red wine. Feeling jolly, I still had the sense to know that I may be slightly over the limit. That's when I did something that I've never done before—I took a cab. Sure enough on the way home, there was a police road block. But, since it was a cab, they waved it past. I arrived home safely without incident. This was a real surprise as I had never driven a cab before, I don't know where I got it and now that it's in my garage, I don't know what to do with it!

(adapted from www.freerepublic.com)

NAÏVE FARMER FROM MINNESOTA

The Minnesota farmer and his favorite gal got married. On their honeymoon trip they were driving to Minneapolis when the farmer put his hand on the gal's knee. Giggling, she said, "You can go furder than 'dat if you vant to." So the farmer drove on to Duluth.

THAT SAME MINNESOTA FARMER

When the Minnesota farmer accidentally dropped 50 cents in the outhouse poop, he immediately threw in his car keys and billfold. He explained to his new wife: "I'm not going doen dere yust for 50 cents."

LONG TERM PLANNING IN OLD RUSSIA

This happened many years ago in the Soviet Socialist Republic. A Russian man saved his rubles for twenty years to buy a new car. After choosing from the limited models of Lada and Skoda, he is not surprised that it will take two years for the new car to be delivered. As he starts to leave the car salesman, he pauses and turns back to the salesman: "Do you know which week two years from now the new car will arrive?" he asks. The salesman tells the man that it will be two years to the exact week. The man thanks the salesman and asks: "Could you possibly tell me what day of the week two years for now the car will arrive?" The salesman, mildly annoyed, checks his notes and says it will be on Thursday. The man thanks the salesman and once again asks: "I'm sorry to be so much trouble, but do you know if that will be two years from now on Thursday in the morning, or the afternoon?" Visibly irritated, the salesman flips through his papers yet another time and says sharply that it will be in the afternoon, two years for now on Thursday, at 2 p.m. "That's a relief," says the man. "The plumber is coming in the morning!"

(adapted from www.orsm.net)

NEEDS A PUSH

A man and his wife were awakened at 3 a.m. by a loud pounding on the door. The man gets up and goes to the door where a drunken stranger, standing in the pouring rain, is asking for a push. "Not a chance," says the husband, "it is 3 a.m. in the morning." He slams the door and returns to bed. "Who was that?" asked his wife. "Just some drunk guy asking for a push," he answers. "Did you help him?" she asks. "No, I did not, it is 3 a.m. in the morning and it is pouring rain out there!" "Well, you have a short memory," says his wife. "Can't you remember about three months ago when we broke down, and those two guys helped us? I think you should help him, and you should be ashamed of yourself!" The man does as he is told, gets dressed, and goes out into the pounding rain. He calls out into the dark, "Hello, are you still there?" "Yes," comes back the answer. "Do you still need a push?" calls out the husband. "Yes, please!" comes the reply from the dark. "Where are you?" asks the husband. "Over here on the swing", replied the drunk.

(adapted from www.petoftheday.com)

WRONG WAY WARREN

Warren III was driving down Route 50 in his yellow Jeep Wrangler "Buttercup", when his car phone rang. Answering, he heard his father, Warren Jr. urgently warning him, "Warren, I just heard on the news that there's a Jeep going the wrong way Route 50. Please be careful!" "I'm on Route 50 now! It's not just ONE car," said Warren III. "It's HUNDREDS of them!"

CROW TALK

They found about 200 dead crows on the highway near Topeka, KS, and so the Federal Government funded a million-dollar study on how they may have died. A Bird Medical Examiner (BME) from the University of Flippabird (U of F) determined that 98% of the crows had been killed by impact with trucks, but only 2% were killed by an impact with a car. The consultant was called in...an Aviary Ornithological Behaviorist (AOB). The AOB and the BME from the U of F determined the cause in short order. When crows eat road kill, they always set up a lookout crow in a nearby tree to warn of impending danger. His conclusion was that the lookout crows could only say "Cah", but none could say "Truck". *(Groan...)*

(adapted from www.veganza.org)

BE SPECIFIC

Two hippie longhairs thoughtfully made a sign saying, "THE END IS NEAR! TURN YOURSELF AROUND NOW BEFORE IT'S TOO LATE!" They showed it to each passing car. One driver who drove by didn't appreciate the sign and shouted at them: "Leave us alone you religious nuts!" All of a sudden the hippies heard a big splash, looked at each other, and one hippie said to the other: "Do you think we should just put up a sign that says 'BRIDGE OUT' instead?"

(adapted from www.nantyglo.com)

LUCKY GAS CAP

A guy filled his car with gas at a self-serve gas station. After he had paid and driven away, he realized that he had left the gas cap on top of his car, and it rolled off his car in the dark. He went back to the gas station to see if he could find another gas cap that would fit. There in a ditch was one, and he tried it on, and it went into place with a satisfying click. "Great," he thought, "I lost my gas cap, but I found another one that fits. And this one's even better because it locks."

(adapted from www.splitcoaststampers.com)

BACK FROM THE DEAD

A taxi passenger tapped the driver on the shoulder to ask him a question. The driver suddenly screamed, lost control of the taxi, went up on the sidewalk, and stopped inches from a shop window. The driver looked back: "Look buddy, don't ever do that again. You scared the daylights out of me!" The passenger apologized and said he didn't realize that a little tap could scare him so much. The driver replied: "Sorry, it's not really your fault. Today is my first day as a cab driver. I've been driving hearses for the last 25 years!!!!!"

(adapted from www.sparkpeople.com)

CRAZY IS NOT STUPID

Hoppy had a flat tire in front of an asylum. As he took the wheel off his car, the nuts that held the wheel on rolled down into the sewer. An inmate looking through the fence observed the incident. "Listen," he suggested, "just take one nut from each of the other three wheels to hold the fourth wheel in place until you can get to the gas station." "Thanks a lot," said Hoppy. "I don't know why you are in that place." The inmate said: "I'm here for being crazy, not for being stupid."

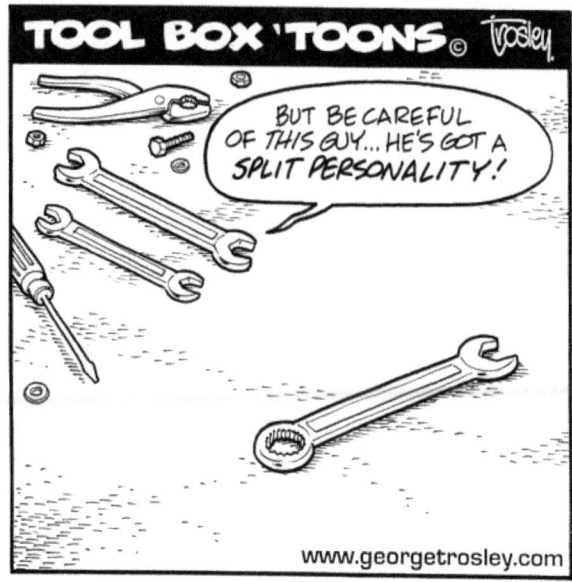

LEAN HOLDER

A young man walked into an insurance office to purchase coverage for his new motorcycle. Only one question from the agent confused him: "Do you have a lien holder on the vehicle?" The biker replied: "I've got a kickstand. Is that the same thing?"

DEVOTION

At the drive-in burger joint, a wife drew her husband's attention to the young couple in the next car, and said, "Do you see those two necking?" "Yes," answered her husband. "See how devoted they are? He kisses that young lady with affection and passion. Why don't you do that?" asked the wife. "I would love to," replied the husband, "but her boyfriend would object."

THE REPLACEMENT

Jethro and his gorgeous girlfriend Cookie cruised every Saturday night in a restored Sunliner owned by Cookie. Jethro usually drove, with Cookie snuggled right up close to him. One night, Jethro died in his sleep. All the guys wondered who Cookie would take up with, who would drive her around in her Sunliner.

Cookie didn't take kindly to guys who wanted to replace Jethro. At the funeral, as they were lowering Jethro into the ground, one eager beaver made his way to Cookie's side. "Cookie," the guy said, "is there a chance that I could take Jethro's place?" "Certainly," Cookie replied, "but you'd better jump in quick; they are about ready to throw dirt on the coffin."

QUIZ: SEVEN Q's AND A's ABOUT OLD CAR GUYS

Question: How many days in a week for a retired guy?

Answer: Six Saturdays to work on the old car, one Sunday for church and a car show.

Question: When is a retiree's bedtime?

Answer: One hour after "Thunder Road" is over on the VCR.

Question: Among old car guys, what is considered formal attire?

Answer: A clean car club T-shirt.

Question: What's the biggest gripe of retirees?

Answer: There is not enough time to air up tires and change the oil in all the cars.

Question: Why are old car guys so slow to clean surplus fenders and extra hoods out of the garage?

Answer: They know that as soon as they do, one of their adult kids will want to store muscle car stuff there.

Question: What is the best way to describe retirement?

Answer: The restoration that never ends.

Question: What do you do all week?

Answer: Monday through Friday, putter with the old Chevy. Saturday and Sunday, I putter some more.

DEER CROSSING

Did you hear about the guy who called the local township administrative office to request the removal of their "DEER CROSSING" sign on the road? The reason:

too many deer were being hit by cars there, and he didn't want the deer to cross there anymore.

(adapted from www.mom2my6pack.com)

TRUE COLORS

Two cab drivers were jabbering at the cab stand. "Hey," asked one cabby, "what's the idea of painting one side of your cab red and the other side blue?" "Well," responded the other cabby, "when I get into an accident, you should see how all the witnesses contradict each other."

(adapted from www.3.telus.net)

MISS DAISY DRIVING

Two elderly ladies were out driving an old 1949 Hudson Commodore, Mildred and Miss Daisy. Mildred in the passenger seat was horrified that Miss Daisy went through a red light. A few minutes later it happened again. She finally spoke up and said, "Miss Daisy, do you realize that you could have gotten us both killed going through those red lights?" Miss Daisy replied, "Oh? Was I driving?"

REALLY HUNGRY

A 1962 Cadillac crashed into a palm tree and got stranded in a remote area of Brazil. Ultimately, the rescue team finds the crashed car. The lone survivor is chewing on a bone, with a huge pile of human bones next to him. The rescuer is shocked. "You can't judge me for this," says the man, "I had to survive!" The leader of the rescue team replies, "But yikes, man…your car only crashed yesterday!"

TOWED OR TOAD?

There once was a Wizard who worked in a factory. Everything was satisfactory except that certain miscreants, taking advantage of his good nature, would steal his parking spot. This continued until he put up the following sign: "THIS PARKING SPACE BELONGS TO THE WIZARD…VIOLATORS WILL BE TOAD?" *(Toad…towed… get it? groan).*

(adapted from www.titysdl.blogspot.com)

SPONTANEOUS COMBUSTION

With global warming and the temperature hitting 100 degrees in several Canadian cities, there have been reports that some Canadian car club guys are spontaneously bursting into flames while they are driving. Talk about hot cars...

STUCK JEEP

The private was driving a jeep down a muddy road and encountered a General whose Jeep was stuck. The private said: "Sir, is your Jeep stuck?" The General tossed the private his keys and said "No, son, yours is!"

OL' BOYS IN LONDON

A group of good ol' boy tourists visit London. They charter a double-decker bus to go to Buckingham Palace, and for some reason all are seated on the upper level. The tour leader, sitting on the bottom, goes up the steps to the top level to see how they're doing. He finds them all sitting tight-lipped, eyes wide open and terrified looks on their faces. Their hands are gripping the seat-backs with white knuckles. "What's wrong with you guys?" he asks. "This is great scenery. Everybody downstairs is enjoying the ride!" "Sure 'nuff", said the good ol' boy in front. "That's because *you* 'uns have a driver!"

CENSUS THE EZ WAY

A small village was totally populated by old car lovers, but they lived in hidden-away places. The census taker did his job the easy way. He simply rolled a wide white Goodyear radial tire down the street marked "For Sale, $10."

SQUIRRELY DRIVER

There's a man trying to cross the street. As he steps off the curb, a car comes screaming around the corner and heads straight for him. The man walks faster, trying to hurry across the street, but the car changes lanes and is still coming at him. So the guy turns around to go back, but the car changes lanes again and is still coming at him. By now, the car is so close and the man so scared that he just freezes and stops in the middle of the road. The car gets real close, then swerves at the last possible moment and screeches to a halt right next to him. The driver rolls down the window. The driver is a squirrel. The squirrel says to the man: "See, it's not as easy as it looks, is it?"

THE HITCHHIKER THIEF?

John was driving late one night when he picked up a hitchhiker. As they rode along he began to become suspicious of his passenger. John checked to see if his wallet was safe in the pocket of his coat that was on the seat between them, but it wasn't there! So he slammed on the brakes, ordered the hitchhiker out, and screamed "Hand over the wallet immediately!" The frightened hitchhiker handed over a billfold, and John drove off. When he arrived home, he started to tell his wife about the experience, but she quickly interrupted him, saying, "Before I forget, John, you left your wallet at home this morning."

UNPREPARED HIGHWAY CREW

One morning, a local highway department crew reached their job-site and realized they had forgotten all their shovels. The crew's foreman radioed the office and told his supervisor of the situation. The supervisor radioed back and said, "Don't worry, we'll send some shovels...just lean on each other until they arrive."

NINE SIGNS THAT YOU'RE GETTING TOO OLD TO DRIVE

1. It takes more than four minutes to get out of your car.

2. When backing into a parking spot, you just back up until you hit something.

3. It scares you to drive the speed limit.

4. The only vehicle you pass on the road anymore is the Amish buggy.

5. You use cruise control because your leg falls asleep.

6. You inquired if the dealership could install magnifying glass for the windshield.

7. Your turn signal has been on since 2004.

8. Your bumper sticker endorses Eisenhower.

9. When the police pull you over, they're surprised to find out you're sober.

GATOR BAIT

Western Tire and Auto Mechanic, Greg, cruised with his 1956 Chrysler New Yorker to his favorite lake and spied two beautiful ladies skinny-dipping. They spotted him and shouted: "We're not getting out until you drive away". Thinking fast, he replied: "OK, but, I'm just here to feed the alligators."

TRUCKER LOSING THE LOAD

As a trucker stops for a red light, a good ol' boy named Horace visiting up North from the Deep South catches up. He jumps out of his car, runs up to the truck, and knocks on the door. The trucker lowers the window, and the ol' boy says, "Hi, my name is Horace and you are losing some of your load." The trucker ignores him and proceeds down the street. When the truck stops for another red light, Horace catches up again, jumps out of his car, runs up and knocks on the window. Again, the trucker lowers the window. Horace hollers; "You are losing some of your load!" Shaking his head, the trucker ignores him again and continues down the street. At the third red light, the same thing happens again. The trucker then tells Horace: "Hey buddy, it's winter In Minnesota, and I'm driving the SALT TRUCK!"

(adapted from www.laffgaff.com)

TELEGRAM

A good ol' boy went to a telegram office, took out a blank form and wrote: "Honk honk honk toot toot toot beep beep beep." The clerk looked at the paper and politely told the guy: "There are only nine words here. You can get ten words for your $5, so you can send another honk or toot or beep for the same price." "But," the ol' boy replied, "That wouldn't make any sense at all!"

HELP!

A man was filling out an application for a truck driver job. A question on the form was: "Who shall we notify in case of a serious accident?"

His answer??? "Anyone in sight, and quickly please!"

SNAIL'S NEW CAR

There was a snail at the car dealer buying a new car. He told the salesman that he wanted to have a custom paint job on his historic Volkswagen bug. He wanted to have a large letter "S" painted over the back of the car. The salesman asked why he wanted such a paint job. The snail replied that when he was driving down the road he wanted everyone to say: "Look at that S car go".

OUTSTANDING FARMER

Kevin, a Mopar guy, is driving down a country road in his 1969 Dodge Super Bee 440 with six-pack, when he spots a farmer standing in the middle of a huge field of grass. He pulls the car over to the side of the road and notices that the farmer is just standing there, doing nothing, looking at nothing. The guy gets out of the car, walks all the way out to the farmer and asks him, "Excuse me mister, but what are you doing?" The farmer replies, "I'm trying to win a Nobel Prize." "How?"

asks the guy, puzzled. "Well, I heard they give the Nobel Prize to people who are out standing in their field."

INSURANCE WRECK

A guy got a refund on his regular insurance bill. The reason? He had a "Wreckless Year of Driving".

THIRTEEN! THIRTEEN! THIRTEEN!

A car nut parks next to an insane asylum-fence and hears chanting from the other side: "Thirteen! Thirteen! Thirteen!", the voices shout. Curious, he peeked through a hole in the fence, and someone from the other side poked him in the eye! The voices then chant: "Fourteen! Fourteen! Fourteen!"

DODGE RAMMED BY ROLLS

Two guys in a Dodge Ram truck were touring England and got rear-ended by a Rolls Royce. Immediately, from the Dodge Ram that got rammed, two huge Americans jump out. Angrily, they go over to the Rolls, pull the guy out on the left side out, and start beating him. He screams: "Come on, guys, stop!" They continue. He tries to stop them again, but they don't listen. Then he says: "Come on, guys, please stop, we are in England!" They answer to him: "We don't care that we are in England, this is how we do things in America, so you are not getting away with it." Then he shouts to them: "Guys, you are bloody idiots, this is England, the driver is in the right seat, the other seat!"

AIR FORCE CASUALTY

There was a bad accident at the Air Force Base. A Jeep ran over a bag of popcorn and killed two kernels. *(Groan)*

ARMY WARGAMES

During an Army war game, a commanding officer's Jeep got stuck in the mud. The C.O. saw some men lounging around nearby and asked them to help him get unstuck. "Sorry sir," said one of the loafers, "but in the wargames, we were listed as ambushed and classified as dead bodies. The rules say we must sit here and do nothing." Enraged, the officer turned to his driver and said, "Go drag a couple of those dead bodies over here and throw them under the wheels to give us some traction." The C.O. got his help...

SUSPECTED OF STEALING

E-1 Private Teko had gate duty at a Marine military base for years. It was his job to make sure that no one drove out of the base with government property and to search exiting vehicles as necessary. Every Friday, a certain suspicious-looking contractor drove out of the base with a pickup truck full of sand. Every Friday, Private Teko he would look in the cab, under the cab, and also poke a pitchfork deeply into the sand. For years, he never found anything. Twenty years later, when both guys were long retired, Private Teko encountered that same contractor, and challenged him: "Look buddy, I never caught you for stealing anything every Friday when you drove those pickups full of sand off the base. But now, the statute of limitations has long-expired, so you can safely tell me what, if anything, you were stealing. So, were you stealing something?" The retired contractor said: "Yep, I was." The former Private Teko said: "Ahah! I knew it! What were you stealing?" The retired contractor replied: "Trucks".

SENIOR SKILLS

A senior citizen said to his eighty-year-old buddy: "So I hear you're getting married?" "Yep!" "Do I know her?" "Nope!" "This woman, is she good looking?" "Not really." "Is she a good cook?" "Nah, she can't cook too well." "Does she have lots of money?" "Nope, poor as a church mouse." "Well then, is she good in bed?" "I don't know." "Why in the world do you want to marry her then?" "Because she can still drive at night!"

AUCTION NEEDS

My friend kept begging me to go to one of those expensive car auctions (like Mecum Auctions) to buy a million dollar car. I made a list of what I would need: (1) someone else's checkbook; and (2) a new friend.

NO DIFFERENCE

Q. Do you know the difference between a Texas tornado and an Alabama divorce?

A. No difference. Either way, somebody loses a trailer.

BIG MIKE

Mike was forgetful, but he still enjoyed making repairs on his Shelby Mustang. So he made a list of five things he wanted to buy for it:

1. Can of engine degreaser

2. Wesley's Bleach White

3. Wheel cover

4. Battery

5. Alternator

Off he went to the Western Tire and Auto. Mike returned home with one can of engine degreaser, two bottles of Wesley's Bleach White, three wheel covers, four batteries, and five alternators.

ONLY MINORS INJURED

A school bus rolled over with 22 children inside.

Fortunately, there were only *minor* injuries...

STUNT MAN

Did you hear about the stunt man who fell over 50 feet but did not hurt himself? Right, he was trying to walk to the back of the bus!

GOT HIS KISS

A man gets on a bus, and ends up sitting up front next to a very attractive lady. Enamored with her, he asks if he can have a kiss. Naturally, she says no, and gets off the bus. The man goes to a passenger behind him and asks him if he knows of a way for him to get a kiss from the attractive lady. "Well," says the passenger, "every night at 8 o'clock, she goes to the church to pray. If you dress up as God, I'm sure you could convince her to kiss you." The man decides to try it, and dresses up in his best God costume, long flowing white robes, gorgeous white beard, and a plastic gold halo. At 8:00 p.m., she sees him. "Oh, it's God!" she exclaims. "Take me with you!" The man tells the lady that she must first kiss him passionately to prove her worthiness. The lady says yes, but tells him she prefers more than just a kiss. Before you know it, they made love. After it's over, the man pulls off his

God disguise, and says: "Ha, ha! I'm the man from the bus!" "Ha, ha!" says the lady, removing her costume. "I'm the guy behind you on the bus!"

LITTLE JEANNIE'S NEW YEAR'S RESOLUTIONS

I will not spit on the floor. I will not make funny faces out the window at other drivers. I will not throw spitballs at others in the vehicle. I will not stick out my tongue and stick my fingers in my ears and wiggle my fingers to anyone. I will not flip a middle finger at anyone on the road. I will not sing vulgar songs on the radio. I will not shout "Shut Up!" to the others around me. I will not do these things because I am the school bus driver!

T-SHIRT SEEN ON JEANNIE THE BUS DRIVER

On the front: I Love Driving My Bus...

On the back: ...When It's Empty!

COMPLAINER

"Every time I get in this vehicle, I get the same seat, I can't see the movie, read comics, and there are no window blinds, so I can't sleep!" The passengers replied, "Shut up and drive the bus!"

TRUE FACT

Instructor: "Auto manufacturers say that it takes 1,000 bolts to hold the modern auto together." Student: "Yep, but only one nut behind the wheel to wreck it!"

IMPULSE BUYER

Did you hear about the New York City guy who suddenly decided to buy a car because he had just found a parking space?

ALL YOUR LIFE?

Tourist (to small-town garage owner): "What a cool retro garage and what a quaint town! Live here all your life?" Garage owner: "Not yet."

BAD LUCK COMES IN THREES

James had always wanted to try parachuting, and so he did, on his 18th birthday. His instructor said: "The main chute will open automatically. There is a reserve chute, and a pickup truck will be waiting to take you back to the airport." Tragically, the main chute did not open. Then the reserve chute did not deploy. James was falling to earth at over 100 MPH, and thought: "Just my luck that the pickup truck won't be there either."

VANITY

A mid-30's lady proud of her figure went to the hardware store to get an extra car key made. She heard the clerk say to her: "You're a model?" Pleased, she primped a bit, and replied: "Why no, I'm not, but thanks for the compliment." The clerk repeated slowly: "Year—and—model?"

SOUTHERN ACCENT

A Yankee fellow flew into Tallahassee airport and attempted to rent a car. The clerk said sweetly: "I have an older accent, is that OK?" The Yankee said: "It's fine. I love a fine old Southern accent, especially when spoken by a Southern belle. I'm from Massachusetts; I'm young, full of vigah and staminer." She replied: "I meant the car. It's a Hyundai Accent!"

SIX WISE WORDS...

1. It's better to always proof-read instructions carefully to see if they any words out.

2. Guy stuck in the mud, to his friend: "I'd move heaven and earth to get out of this mudhole." Friend: "Try heaven, you've already moved most of the earth."

3. Buckle up. It makes it harder for the aliens to snatch you from your car.

4. If all your troubles are behind you, you're probably a school bus driver.

5. The fastest way to find a lost tool is to buy its replacement.

6. We'll always be best friend car buddies because you know too much.

COULD NOT AFFORD THE CADDY

I bought me a new car. A big, long and wide black Cadillac convertible. It had a push-button transmission, rolled and pleated interior, all the power options you could buy and more horsepower than you could ever use. Big, wide whitewall tires, fancy wire wheels, a continental kit, dual spotlights, two antennae, skirts, the latest stereo with ten speakers, fold-down seats and everything on the dash was chrome. Here's the best part: the ladies loved it! And so did I. I was a king in my mobile castle. Then one month I fell behind in my payments. I never had a car with payments so high. Insurance on that car was through the roof and that sucker sure could drink up the high test gasoline. The combination of all these problems led to the inevitable: repossession. Now I just sit around dreaming about the good ol' days with all those ladies and that fancy car... If I ever get enough money to buy another car, I'm gonna buy a car I can afford, and I do mean A FORD. (by Ken "Scissorhands" Colbert, and inspired by a Chuck Berry tune).

AND SPEAKING OF HUMOROUS CAR SONGS....

A great website (https://spinditty.com/playlists/Zero-to-Sixty-Playlist-Pop-Rock-Country-Songs-About-Cars) lists "129 Songs About Cars and Driving", and many of these have humorous lyrics. This big topic merits a different book. However, a few of my personal funny favorites are: "The Corvette Song (The One I Loved Back Then)" by George Jones; "Fun, Fun, Fun" by the Beach Boys; "Mercedes Benz" by Janis Joplin; "Mustang Sally" by Wilson Pickett; "Little Deuce Coupe" by the Beach Boys; "Greased Lightning" by John Trevolta; "Thunder Road" by Robert Mitchum; "Hot Rod Lincoln" by Charlie Ryan; "One Piece at a Time" by Johnnie Cash; "Tell Laura I Love Her" by Ray Peterson; "The Little Old Lady From Pasadena" by Jan and Dean; "Beep Beep" by the Playmates; "Rapid Roy (The Stock Car Boy)"; and last but best, "Paradise by the Dashboard Lights" by Meat Loaf. How many do you know?

FROG REQUESTS LOAN

A frog hopped in to a bank and approached the teller. Her nameplate says that her name is Patty Whack. The frog says: "Miss Whack, I'd like to get a $30,000 loan to buy a restored 1988 Camaro Iroc Z-28 convertible." Patty looks askance at the frog and asks his name. The frog says that his name is Hoppy Jagger and that his father is Mick Jagger, who, he brags, knows the bank manager personally. Patty explains that he will need to secure the loan with some collateral. The frog says, "Sure. I have this," and produces a 2" die cast 1956 pink Ford matchbox car replica like Dale Earnhardt used to drive. Patty takes the tiny car and goes off to consult with the bank manager. She finds the manager and says, "There's a frog named Hoppy Jagger out there who claims to know you and wants to borrow $30,000, and he wants to use this tiny car replica as collateral. And what is this little car?" The bank manager tells her he knows the frog and everything is OK: "It's a knick-knack, Patty Whack. Give the frog a loan. His old man's a Rolling Stone."

(adapted from www.mikeysFunnies.com)

KILLED THE GOAT

Nancy Pelosi (Dem.) and Mitch McConnell (Rep.) mended political fences because they had just cosponsored a bill to require that everyone must drive electric cars. They were driving through a small country town in her V-12 Hummer when Nancy accidentally hit and killed a sorry looking old goat. Mitch encouraged her to go to the nearby farmhouse and apologize. Nancy got up her nerve and knocked on the front door, and the farmer let her in. She was in there for a whole hour. When Nancy came out, Mitch was perplexed about why she had been in there so long. Nancy explained that the farmer shook her hand, offered her wine, and his wife gave her cookies. Mitch asked: "What did you tell the farmer?" Nancy replied: "I just told him I was driving around with Mitch McConnell and I had just killed the old goat."

CAMPAIGN PROMISE

A fellow was running for Mayor of Detroit. His campaign promise was: "I promise to bring back to America robot jobs that have long been lost to foreign robots!"

(adapted from The American Legion Magazine, April 2020)

THE SENTRY

A new soldier was on sentry duty at the main gate of an Army base. His orders were clear: no car was to enter unless it had a special sticker on the windshield. A large Army Hummer pulled up with a general seated in the back. The sentry said,

"Halt, who goes there?" The chauffeur, a corporal, said, "General Smith is next to me." The sentry said sternly: "I can't let you through, corporal. You've got to have a sticker on the windshield." The general said gruffly, "Drive on, corporal!" The sentry quickly raised his rifle and took off the safety: "Hold it! You really can't come through. I have orders to shoot if you try driving in without a sticker." The gruff general again ordered his driver: "I'm telling you, son, drive on!" The sentry aimed his rifle at them, finger on the trigger, hand shaking, and said: "General, I'm new at this. Do I shoot you or the driver?"

(adapted from The American Legion Magazine, April 2020)

LOST IN THE BIG CITY

Paul went to the big city and got lost, so he called Cecil for help. Cecil asked Paul to look up and see what street he was on and Paul replied, "I'm on the corner of walk and don't walk."

HOW TO SAVE MONEY

Travis (panting, out of breath, to his wife): "I missed the bus trying to get home today. So I ran behind it all the way home."

Travis' Wife: "So???" Travis said: "So I saved 95 cents!"

Travis (with a big grin): "Yep. So tomorrow I'm a goin' to miss a taxi and save $10!"

FOUND ONE

Finn was driving down the big city street in a sweat because he had an important meeting and couldn't find a parking place... Looking up to heaven he said, "Lord, take pity on me. If you find me a parking place, I will go to Mass every Sunday for the rest of me life and give up me Irish Whiskey." Miraculously, a parking place appeared. Finn looked up again and said, "Never mind, Lord, I found me one!"

RIGHT-OF-WAY

Q: Who has the right-of-way when four cars approach a four-way stop at the same time?

A: The pickup truck with the gun rack and the bumper sticker saying, "Guns don't kill people. I do."

LATE, EARLY, WHATEVER...

After she finished her route, Jeannie the school bus driver had to explain to her supervisor why she was 10 minutes late: "I was stuck behind a big truck," said Jeanne. "Okay, but yesterday you were 10 minutes EARLY!" reminded the boss. "Yes, but yesterday I was following a hot rod!"

CHAPTER SIXTEEN

CRUISERS AT THE WATERING HOLE

Watering holes are bars, cafes, cantinas, dram shops, gin mills, grogshops, pubs, saloons, taprooms, and/or taverns. The Webster dictionary defines "watering hole" as "...a bar, nightclub, or other social gathering place where alcoholic drinks are sold." Jokesters always begin with "a man walked into a bar", and we immediately grin. Add to that grin our automotive punch lines and you will grin twice!

MILD-MANNERED TRUCK DRIVER

Steve was a long-haul semi-driver who hauled six cars at a time on his rig. He stopped at the 2A Roadside Bar for lunch. Steve ordered a cheeseburger, coffee, and a slice of apple pie. As he was about to eat, three Harley soft-tail motorcycles pulled up outside. The bikers came in, and one grabbed the trucker's cheeseburger and took a bite from it. The second one drank the trucker's coffee, and the third wolfed down the apple pie. Steve didn't say a word. He simply got up, paid the cashier, and left. When he was gone, one of the motorcyclists said, "He ain't much of a man, is he?" "He's not much of a driver, either," the cashier replied. "He just drove his 18 wheeler truck over three motorcycles."

(adapted from www.globalchristiancenter.com and www.laffgaff.com)

ENGINE RUNNING

The Lone Ranger and Tonto were in a bar drinking a beer when a cowboy walked in and said "Who owns the big white horse outside?" The Lone Ranger said, "I do…Why?" The cowboy said, "I just thought you'd like to know that your horse is overheated and just about dead!" The Lone Ranger and Tonto rushed outside and sure enough, Silver was ready to die from heat exhaustion. He got the horse some water and soon Silver was starting to feel a little better. Tonto then volunteered to help, saying; "Kemosabe, you go in and enjoy your beer and I will run 'round and 'round Silver and make a breeze to help cool him off." The Lone Ranger returned to the bar to finish his drink. A few minutes later, another cowboy struts into the bar and asks, "Who owns that big white horse outside?" The Lone Ranger stands again, and claims, "I do, what's wrong with him this time?" The cowboy looks him in the eye and says: "Nothing, but you left your Injun' runnin'!" *(Get it? Engine running?)*

(adapted from www.jokesarena.com)

ABSOLUTELY POSITIVE

A car battery walks into a bar. He says to the bartender that he thinks he lost his car keys somewhere in the bar. The bartender asks: "Are you sure?" The battery replies: "I'm positive!"

A BENDER

Two drunks decided to go on a three-day binge, a "bender". They took the car, and guess what? They had a fender bender.

GOOD ACTOR

A fellow walked out of a bar, to the parking lot, dropped his keys, picked them up, staggered a bit, dropped his keys again, unlocked his car, got in, all while being watched by a suspicious police officer. The fellow heard a "tap, tap, tap" on his window, and he rolled it down. "License, registration, and blow into this breathalyzer please," said the cop. The fellow complied, but to the officer's surprise, the breathalyzer registered 0.0 in the fellow's system. The officer asked why he staggered so often leaving the bar. The fellow replied: "To fool all my drunken friends inside the bar. They all would have wanted rides home."

TOO DRUNK TO...

Three happy drunks were getting ready to leave the bar. They staggered to the pick 'em up truck and pushed Alex into the driver's seat. Alex was in the worst shape of all. They told Alex: "You drive. You're too drunk to sing."

JUDGE'S VERDICT

The judge proclaimed: "Po' Boy: the jury has found that there is insufficient evidence to find you guilty of car theft."

Po' Boy replied: "You mean I am free to go?"

Judge: "Yes. You are free to go."

Po' Boy: "Does this mean I get to keep the car?"

HOLY DRINK

A priest drives his Cadillac Eldorado to the Noplace Bar and walks in. He tells the bartender: "I'll have my usual, vodka and holy water." The bartender says: "I'm new. What do they call that drink?" The priest says: "A Holy Spirit."

GOOD ADVICE

Don't drink and drive, it will spill and mess up the seats and stain your carpets.

BETTER ADVICE

If you drink, drive, don't park, because accidents cause people.

BEST ADVICE

Bartenders shouldn't cut people off. They should get them so drunk that they can't find their keys.

BIG WHEEL

Did you hear about the guy that started drinking so young that his first DWI was on a Big Wheel?

GOOD QUESTION

If you can't drink and drive, why do you need a driver's license to buy alcohol?

(adapted from www.jokes4us.com) (for this and the five jokes above)

NEW DIET

Shawn decided to lose weight on the new wine and beer diet. He lost 10 pounds and his driver's license!

TENNESSEE ENGINEERING EXAM

Question: If Calvin built a still that operates at a capacity of 20 gallons of 'shine per hour, how many car radiators are necessary to condense the product?

Answer: If Calvin knows, shame on him! Also, he is probably under ATF surveillance.

(adapted from www.bitoffun.com)

GOOD OL' BOYS BET

Two good ol' boys meet in a bar for a beer. The 7:00 evening news is on TV and there is footage of Robbie Kneivel about to jump his motorcycle from one sky-scraper roof across the street and land on the other skyscraper roof.

Ol' boy #1 says, "I'll bet you $20 he crashes and burns."

Ol' boy #2 says, "I will take your bet, I think he will make the jump OK." Minutes later, Robbie jumps, misses his landing, crashes and burns."

Ol' boy #2 opens his wallet to give ol' boy #1 the $20.

Ol' boy #1 says, "I can't take your money. I cheated. I saw this an hour ago on the 6:00 news."

Ol' boy #2 replies, "Well honestly, I saw it too. But I didn't think for a second that Robbie would do it again."

(adapted from www.funny-jokes-quotes-sayings.com)

FAVORITE DRINK

A lady's gynecologist friend drove her to his favorite bar in his new Lincoln and ordered his favorite drink which he invented, a shooter with Pabst beer and Smirnoff vodka. It's called a "Pabst Smir."

UNGRATEFUL

A Ford guy walks into his favorite bar and runs into a young acquaintance looking very sad.

"Is there anything wrong?" asked the Ford guy.

"Two months ago my grandfather died and left me his collection of vintage Morgans," said the guy.

"That doesn't sound like anything to be upset about," said the Ford guy. "It should happen to me."

"Yeah," said the young guy, "but last month an uncle on my father's side passed away. He left me his muscle car museum."

"So why are you sitting here looking so unhappy?"

Said the young guy: "This month, so far, not a cent."

(adapted from www.retributionscaveforumotion.com)

JUMPER CABLE IN A BAR

A jumper cable walks into a bar. The bartender says, "I'll serve you but don't start anything."

(adapted from www.nie/senhayden.com)

ASPHALT IN A BAR

A man walks into a bar with a slab of asphalt pavement under his arm and says: "A beer for me please, and one more for the road."

(adapted from www.jokersrevenge.com)

QUIT WHILE YOU'RE AHEAD

A guy named John Young walks into a bar holding a human head. The head smiles and winks at the bartender. John says to the bartender: "I'll have a beer, and another brew for my friend, Dave the head." Dismayed, the bartender serves up two beers. As Dave the head finishes his beer, out pops a body to hold the head. Another beer later, out pops an arm. Three more beers later, the other arm plus two legs! Dave the head is overjoyed, and runs out into the street, shouting: "I'm whole again! I'm whole again!" However, a speeding Jeep Cherokee runs him over, flattening him. The moral of the story? "QUIT WHILE YOU'RE A HEAD."

(adapted from www.jokersrevenge.com)

SMALL COMPLIMENTS

A good ol' boy drove to a bar in his flat black rat rod 1949 Hudson and walked in. The car's vanity tag said: "LDIABLO". As he walked in to a nearly empty bar, a voice said: "I really dig that custom hood ornament on your car, the chrome devil with ruby eyes and sharp fangs." The ol' boy looked around and saw no one. Then another little voice said: "Atta boy, I really like the wide whites and full moons". Again, he saw no one. Then another little voice chirped: "I loved the sound of that 360 engine rumbling through those glass packs!" The ol' boy found the bartender and asked about the voices. The bartender said: "It's not me. It's the complimentary peanuts!"

CHAPTER SEVENTEEN

CRUISIN' AND MAN'S BEST FRIEND

Unquestionably, man's best friend is his dog. As anyone who has one can testify, dogs not only understand us, but they also have uncanny understandings of the ways that vehicles affect our (and their) lives. Find out how! Bow wow! Now!

A DALMATIAN'S PURPOSE

Three kids were walking home when a firetruck zoomed past. Sitting proudly in the front seat was a Dalmatian. The oldest little boy guessed they used the dog to keep people back from the fire. His sister said no, she thought the Dalmatian is to guide them to people who were caught in the fire and needed to be rescued. Their little brother said they were both wrong. "They use the dog," he said, "to help them find the fire hydrant."

WATSON, THE CATHOLIC DOG

"Crocodile Kilby" was an Australian fellow who enjoyed cruising with his dog in his mid-50's Ford Ute. (A Ute is like a Ranchero or El Camino). Watson's ears would flop in the wind and he would sit with authority in the Ute's open bed, bark happily at the dogs they passed, and sniff the fresh air. Alas, sadly. Watson died, and Croc wanted to give him a proper religious service as he passed into doggie heaven. After all, Croc thought that Watson was better than most people. So Croc approached Father O'Brien, the parish priest. He asked for a high mass, full choir, six altar candles—the works. Father O'Brien said: "I'm sorry, we just cannot do a high mass funeral for a dog." So Croc said to Father O'Brien: "I wonder if the Vicar at the Episcopalian Church across town would do a proper service for my dog for a $5,000 donation?" Father O'Brien's eyes lit up: "Hold it right there, Croc, you didn't tell me your dog was a Catholic..."

NUTHIN' BUT A HOUND DOG

Good Ol' Boy: "Guess what? I taught my hound dog to drive my car!"

Buddy: "Wow. He must be really smart!"

Good Ol' Boy: "Not so. He already has three speeding tickets!"

ARF!

Q. Where do dogs park their cars?

A. In the barking lot.

TWELVE REASONS TO CRUISE WITH YOUR DOG RATHER THAN WITH YOUR WIFE

1. Dogs think you're more fun when you drive drunk.

2. If you notice a beautiful dog, you won't get jabbed in the ribs.

3. If a dog sniffs another dog on you, he just thinks it's interesting.

4. If you cruise alone and come home late, the dog is even happier to see you.

5. If you call your dog by the wrong name, he is not bothered by it.

6. When you go out to eat, your dog is happy with table scraps.

7. When you ride with your convertible top down, your dog likes to muss his hair in the wind.

8. Your dog's parents will never visit and chide you about how much money you waste on old cars.

9. Dogs love to go with you when you go hunting or fishing.

10. Your dog will not wake you in the middle of the night and ask: "If I died, would you get another dog?"

11. If your dog has babies, you can run an ad in the paper and sell them.

12. If your dog leaves you, he won't take half of your stuff.

(adapted from www.gameboomers.com; and www.city-data.com)

ELEVEN REASONS WHY WOMEN SHOULD CRUISE WITH THEIR DOGS RATHER THAN WITH THEIR HUSBANDS

1. If you notice a good-looking man, dogs don't feel insecure or jealous.

2. Dogs don't advise you on how to drive, step on an imaginary brake, and don't care if you take too long to merge into heavy traffic.

3. Dogs are always eager to cruise with you, no matter what kind of car you drive.

4. Dogs don't care if your face is not made up, you hair is messy, or if you shave your legs. They just want to CRUISE!

5. If you cruise without your dog, he will still be happy to see you when you come home.

6. You can make your dog take a bath and smell nice before you let him get in the car.

7. Dogs don't criticize your mother, other relatives, or friends while you are driving.

8. Dogs don't mind if you do all the driving or if you drive drunk or stoned, as long as meal times are not delayed.

9. Dogs don't hold back on their emotions—they cry, wag their tails, bark happily, feel ashamed.

10. Your dog won't give you a social disease if you take him to a drive-in movie.

11. You won't be totally embarrassed if your dog pees on the tire of your car.

(suggested by Jennifer Berman's book "Why Dogs Are Better Than Men." Andrews McMeel Publishing, 2001.)

WATCHDOGS

An old boy fired up his Ford truck and went hunting, and ran into his buddy Homer. Homer had two new dogs, so the old boy asked what their names were. Homer replied that their names were Timex and Casio. The old boy said, "Why would anyone name dogs' that-a-way?" "DUHHHHH......," answered Homer,"They're *watch* dogs!"

(adapted from www.kidzworld.com)

BEAGLE DRIVER

A beagle walks into a job center. "Wow, a talking dog," says the clerk. "With your talent I'm sure we can find you a gig in the circus." "The circus?" says the beagle. "What would the circus want with a professional race car driver?"

GOOD OL' BOYS AT CAVERN IN MASSACHUSETTS

Two Good Ol' Boys, Jim and Jay, from Lynn, Massachusetts are out hunting exotic plants, and as they are walking along they come upon a huge cavern in the ground, and its bone dry and very deep and dark. They approach it and are amazed by the size of it. Jim says, "Wow, that's some hole. I can't even see the bottom. I wonder how deep it is." "I don't know," Jay says. "Let's throw something down and listen and see how long it takes to hit bottom." "There's this old Fordomatic transmission here," Jim says. "Give me a hand and we'll throw it in and see." So they pick it up and carry it to the hole. They count one, two, three and heave it in the hole. They are standing there listening and looking over the edge and then they hear a rustling in the brush behind them. As they turn around they see a huge brown hound dog come crashing through the brush. It heads straight to the hole and, with no hesitation, dives in head first. They are standing there looking at each other puzzled, looking in the hole and trying to figure out what that was all about. Then an old farmer walks up. "Say there," says the farmer: "You fellers didn't happen to see my big brown hound dog around here anywhere, did you?" "Funny you should ask," Jim says. "We were just standing here a minute ago and a big brown hound dog came crashing through the bushes doin' about a hunnert miles an hour and jumped headfirst into this hole here." "That's impossible," the old farmer says: "I had him chained to an old Fordomatic transmission!"

(Note: Jay Leno has a version of this joke with an anvil and a goat). (adapted from jokeswarehouse.com)

BLIND DRIVER TERRORS

Question: Why don't blind people drive their cars more often?

Answer: Because it terrorizes their Seeing Eye dogs.

DRIVING TO THE FLEA MARKET

A very talented dog loved to drive his master's car, but the master needed his car to go to work Monday through Friday. So the dog was allowed to drive his friends to the flea market on Saturdays.

LAZY DOG

Q: How can you tell if you have a lazy dog?

A: It chases parked cars!

LITTERING

A pregnant female dog gave birth at the side of the road. She got fined for littering.

DEFINITION

Dog Kennel: A barking lot!

(Note: previous three jokes, see www.rd.com)

VERY LAZY DOG

"I tell ya, my dog is lazy; he don't chase cars. He sits on the curb and takes down license plate numbers." --Rodney Dangerfield

WHY DO DOGS CHASE CARS?

Why do men chase women that they have no intention of marrying? For the same reason that dogs chase cars that they have no intention of driving!

(adapted from www.womansavers.com)

CHAPTER EIGHTEEN

WIT AND WISDOM

Wisdom includes abiding by accepted mottos, rules, widespread beliefs, brilliant thoughts, answers to the big questions in life, important lessons which people learn the hard way, and/or obedience to a Dad's directives. Wisdom can include adherence to Chinese proverbs or government directives (or else!). Even car club newsletter editors have rules to obey and hence must exhibit wisdom to their readers versed in proper English, southern slang, car talk, redneck slang, and good ol' boy lingo. Ridiculous riddles, rules, rejoinders, rigmarole, riprap, rollickings and rubrics for auto aficionados.

POSITION MATTERS

Q. What is the difference between a Harley motorcycle and a Hoover vacuum cleaner?

A. The size of the dirt bag!

EPA SEZ

EPA says: "Air pollution is a mist-demeanor."

SUCCESS

"The road to success is lined with many tempting parking spaces."

(www.famouslifemottos.org)

CONSOLATION

Wealthy people who pay all-cash for a car miss one of life's really big thrills: Making the last car payment!

DRIVER'S LICENSE QUESTION

What hair color do they put on the driver's license of a bald man?

TEENAGE DATE

When I was in high school, I got in trouble with my girlfriend's father. He said, "I want my daughter back by 8:15." I said, "Great! The middle of August? Cool."

A WHITE SPORT COAT AND...

If everyone in the USA drove a pink car we would be a pink car nation.

CAR CLUB MAGAZINE WAS Y2K READY

The car club magazine was Y2K ready, and finished converting the months on all of the club calendars such that "Y" has been changed to "K". The year 2000 months became as follows: Januark, Februark, Mak, Julk. The other months are alright since they do not have a "Y" to change to a "K".

RENT-A-WRECK

Q. What's the difference between a Rent-A-Wreck rental car and a Jeep?

A. The Rent-A-Wreck car is driven in places you wouldn't even take a Jeep.

BOLL THE LESSER

Two boll weevils grew up in South Carolina. One built Mopar muscle cars with big motors. The other stayed behind in the cotton fields and never amounted to much. The second one, naturally, became known as the lesser of two weevils.

(adapted from www.scrapgirls.net)

FIVE CHINESE PROVERBS

1) "Man who run in front of car get tired"

2) "Man who run behind car get exhausted"

3) "Man who drive like hell, bound to get there!"

4) "Two wrongs not make a right. Three lefts do."

5) "The man with six children will always be happier than the man with six classic cars because the man with the cars always wants more."

DEMON'S BILL

Roger had a Model A Ford which he planned to make into a stylish hot rod. He hired "Demon" of Hot Rod Garage to design it for $5,000. Only two days later, Demon presented his design to Roger with his bill for $5,000. Roger protested: "$5,000 for two days' work?" Demon replied: "Not for two days, but for the relevant educational experiences of my entire life."

GOOD HIT

At the end of a car show at the local high school one evening, Jay's '58 Edsel refused to start. How to get home? In a frantic call to Western Auto, as the manager was closing up, Jay convinced Doby the manager to come to his rescue. Doby opened the hood, and asked for a hammer. Doby then stalked around Jay's engine, intent on determining the problem. Finally, he stopped, and lightly tapped the relay. Jay turned the key and the Edsel started immediately, so Doby presented Jay with a bill for $305. Jay protested: "$305 just for tapping the relay with a hammer?" "No," said Doby, "Five dollars for the tap, but $300 for knowing *where* to tap."

SOLUTION

Did you hear about the old car enthusiast who read about the connection between touching used motor oil and finger cancer? He convinced himself to stop reading.

BETTER NEXT TIME?

Restoring old cars is a lot like raising children. You keep thinking you'll do better next time.

CAR WASH

There are two ways to get your car clean and shiny. The five-minute car wash is when machines do it. Then there's the five-week car wash. That's when you ask your kids to do it.

THIN TIRES

Modern tires are tall and thin. They used to worry about nails. Now they worry about mosquitos!

GUN IT

With most cars, you want to gun the engine. With this car, you want to use the gun *on* it!

POOR HOUSE

Have you seen the price tags for hopped-up supercharged cars? They can get you where you're going—the poorhouse!

MOVING UP?

Did you hear about the guy who went to Las Vegas with a $50,000 Corvette and came home in a $300,000 Greyhound bus?

DANGER

An old Ford can be a very dangerous place. Ask any girl who's ever parked the backseat of one!

USED CAR DEALER BUSINESS ETHICS

Schwartz's young hopeful at the used car dealership, Danny, asked one day, "Dad, what do they mean when they say 'business ethics'?" Dad beamed. "Very good question, my son. Let us assume a woman comes into the store, orders a $25,000 car and places $30,000 on the counter. You make the change, which comes to $5,000 and turn to take care of your other customers. A few minutes later you become aware that she has left the store but has forgotten to take her $5,000 in change, which remains on the counter. Do you see the picture, my son?" "Yes, Dad." "Now comes the question of business ethics," Schwartz said. "Do I, or do I not, tell my partner?"

HOW ARE YOU PARKED?

Ever feel like you're diagonally parked in a parallel universe?

DISASTER WISDOM?

A Ford guy, a Chevy guy, and a Yugo guy (yes, there are a few left) went touring in Iran but were mistakenly arrested as spies. They were backed up to a wall facing a firing squad. The Ford guy was stood by the wall, and just as the soldiers were about to fire, he yelled: "Earthquake!" The firing squad hit the deck, and the Ford guy jumped over the wall and escaped. Next, the Chevy guy was stood against the wall. Seeing how the Ford guy's trick worked, he screamed: "Tornado!" The firing squad ran to a nearby basement and he escaped. The Yugo guy had it all figured out. He would scream about an impending disaster, the cowardly firing squad soldiers will run away, and he would escape over the wall. So just as the rifles were aimed at him, the Yugo guy shouted as loud as he could: "Fire!"

THE KEY TO SUCCESS

At a car show, a guy who owned a beautiful Rolls Royce was heard boasting to a Ford truck guy: "You can buy any magnificent vehicle you wish in life if your parents worked hard enough."

WISDOM, GOOD LOOKS, OR A CAR

Years ago, an angel appeared at the Cruiser Car Club meeting and told the President Jimmy that in return for his unselfish and exemplary behavior, the Lord will reward him with his choice of infinite wisdom, great looks, or a restored 1969 GTO. Without hesitating, President Jimmy selected infinite wisdom. "Done!" said the angel, who disappeared in a cloud of smoke and a bolt of lightning. Now, all heads turn toward President Jimmy, who sat surrounded by a faint halo of light, looking wiser. One of his colleagues whispered, "Say something." The President sighed and said, "Now that I'm wiser, I think I should have taken the car."

THREE LIFE QUESTIONS

1) Why is the time of day with the slowest traffic called rush hour?

2) Do you think Houdini ever locked his keys in the car?

3) Why is there a road sign that says "Braille Institute, Next Exit"?

TURTLE ROAD QUIZ

Q: Why did the turtle cross the road?

A: To get to the Shell station.

MONSTER ROAD QUIZ

Q: What do monsters make with cars?

A: Traffic jam.

TWO NEW YORK CITY DRIVING RULES

1. Never stop for a pedestrian unless he is under the wheels of your car.

2. Always look both ways when running a red light.

Q. AND A.: CHICKEN COUPES

Q. Why do chicken coops only have two doors?

A. Because if they had four, they would be chicken sedans!

Q. AND A.: PAPER CAR BODIES?

Q. Do you know why they don't make car bodies out of paper?

A. Because they would be tearable! *(Groan)*

NOT YET DEAD

Whenever we drive past a graveyard, my dad says, "Do you know why I can't be buried there?" And I'd say, "Why not?" And dad says, ""'Because I'm not dead yet!"

TWO-TIRED

Q. Do you know why motorcycles can't stand up on their own?

A. Because they are two-tired!

Q. AND A.: PAST YOUR EYES

Q. Why do milk trucks drive so fast that they are hard to see?

A. Because they are all pasteurized before you spot them. *(Get it, past-your-eyes...groan).*

LET'S BOOGIE

Q. How do little kids improve an old car's music system?

A. Just put a little boogie In the seat!

TURN YOURSELF AROUND

Q. Did you hear about the car thief who was addicted to the hokey pokey?

A. Fortunately, he turned himself around.

EMBARRASSED

Q. What did the green traffic light say to the red traffic light?

A. Don't look. I'm changing.

DOWN IN HISTORY

Q. Did you hear about the McPherson College Automotive class student who fainted while studying Daytona races?

A. Yep, he went down in automotive history.

SIX MOTTOS TO LEARN

1. My mechanic always gives 100%...12% Monday; 23% Tuesday; 40% Wednesday; 24% Thursday; 1% Friday.

2. Man cannot live by bread alone. He also needs a roll of duct tape and a can of WD-40.

3. One nice thing about being over the hill is that you begin to pick up speed.

4. The tire is only flat on the bottom.

5. VENI, VEDI, VISA: I came, I saw, I shopped for car parts on my credit card.

6. Sign in a car dealership office: "The best way to get back on your feet – miss a car payment."

(adapted from www.hackthissite.org)

MATH QUESTION?

Question: You're driving a bus with 43 people from Chicago, stop in Pittsburgh, and pick up seven people and drop off five, pick up four more in Cleveland and drop off eight. Upon arriving in Philadelphia 20 hours later, what's the driver's name? *(Think about it).*

(ANSWER: Your name. You're the driver!)

COLLISION, ACCIDENT, ETC...

A '55 Ford ran into a truck loaded with thousands of copies of Roget's Thesaurus... according to the newspaper, witnesses were stunned, startled, aghast, taken aback, stupefied.

(adapted from www.literacyla.org)

IF I HAD A DOLLAR...

If I had a dollar for every girl that found me unattractive, eventually they would find me attractive. And if I took those dollars and bought a red 1969 Cadillac Eldorado convertible, they would find me MUCH more attractive.

IF MY BODY WAS A CAR

If my body was a car, I would have traded it in long ago. I have bumps and dents and scratches and deep pits in my chrome. My headlights are out of focus and I can't see things up close or far away. My traction is terrible; I wobble and bump along even in good weather. My once-beautiful wide whites are now stained with varicose veins. My maximum speed is much lower than before. I need additives for my fuel...called vitamins and prescription drugs. Every time I cough or sputter, my exhaust backfires. No one can handle the total restoration it needs. I would like to trade it in, but nobody wants it except the boneyard.

POWDER COATING INSTRUCTION

When you powder coat your carburetor, get all the gas out before you cure it in a microwave oven.

BAD GUESS

Two West Virginia hillbillies are driving their old pickups down a dusty street and stop, nose to nose. The hillbillies jump out to greet each other. Hoppy is carrying a sack. Tommy Ray says, "Hey Hoppy, what'cha got in the bag?" Hoppy sez: "Jus' some chickens." Tommy Ray says: "If I guesses how many they are, can I have one?" Hoppy sez: "Shoot, if 'ya guesses right I'll give you BOTH of them." Tommy Ray says: "OK. I guess five."

ALCOHOLISM PREVENTION?

Did you hear that they have raised the minimum drinking age in West Virginia to 32? It seems they want to keep alcohol out of the grade schools!

HEE HAW

Question: What do they call reruns of "Hee Haw" in West Virginia?

Answer: A documentary?

NINE BRILLANT THOUGHTS OF CAR GUYS

1. Good motto for guys who modify old cars: "Do not believe in miracles...rely on them."

2. Women would get along better with their car guy husbands better if they realized that men have feelings, too. For example, they sometimes feel hungry.

3. From fellows who drive 30's cars: "We don't have gray hair. We have 'wisdom highlights'."

4. From typical car club guy: "I'm going to retire, work on old cars, and live off of my savings...not sure what I'll do the second month."

5. Experienced drivers know: "If you lined up all the cars in the world end to end, some idiot would try to pass on a hill with double solid lines."

6. "Last year I joined the Procrastinators Car Club, but we haven't met yet."

7. "Life isn't about how fast you drive, or how high a hill you can climb; it's about how well you restart."

8. Would there be fewer accidents if the manufacturers give their car models less aggressive names, such as **Baby Mustang, Bunny Rabbit,** and **Feather Duster?**

9. Want to live longer? Drive defensively... Buy a tank!

TEN UGLY TRUTHS

1. We live in a society where pizza is delivered to your house in a faster car than the ones that the police drive.

2. If you think nobody cares if you're alive, try missing a car payment.

3. Going to church doesn't make you a Christian any more than standing in a garage makes you a car.

4. The shinbone is a device for finding an open drawer in your Snap-On tool chest in the dark.

5. Behind every successful man is a loving woman. Behind the fall of a successful man is usually a woman who doesn't understand his latest old car.

6. Only crush *ugly* old cars. They have nothing to lose.

7. It's not the driving that kills you; it's the sudden stop at the end.

8. My mechanic told me my motor was fried and I said I want a second opinion. He said okay, your transmission is toast as well.

9. I used to be indecisive between hardtops and convertibles. Now, I'm not sure.

10. A bus is a vehicle that runs twice as fast when you are chasing it as when you are in it.

(adapted from www.dhammawheel.com)

TEN ANNOYING TRUTHS

1, It will always cost more than you think.

2. The engine never makes as much power as you think it should. The corollary to this is: Your car is always slower than you think.

3. There will forever be someone with a bigger motor, a better paint job, or a quicker e.t.

4. A universal part universally doesn't fit anything.

5. The shortest distance between two brake-line fittings is never a straight line. If it is, you've obviously overlooked the inherent flaw.

6. When dropped, the nut will always fall into the least accessible spot. If you're especially gifted, the nut will drop down the intake manifold!

7. Your newly discovered trick part never works when your friends (or investors) are watching.

8. Those "wonder" mechanics-in-a-can chemicals are aptly named—you wonder why you keep trying them because they never work!

9. There will always be hot rodders who can break the unbreakable.

10. And finally, if it sounds too good to be true—it probably is. And it will still cost more than you think!

JEEP STATISTIC

Jeeps are very hardy, and 98% of all Jeeps ever made are still rolling over rocks and through loose sand. (Unfortunately, only 2% have ever made it home.)

PRICKS

Q. What is the difference between a porcupine and a Rolls Royce?

A. With a Rolls Royce, the pricks are on the *inside*.

RIDDLE 1492

Do you know which "bus" crossed the Atlantic Ocean? Christopher Colum-bus!

NINE WAYS YOU KNOW YOU BOUGHT A LEMON

1. As you leave the used car lot, you see the dealership's owner rush out with a gigantic smile and high-five the salesman.

2. You notice that the car phone they threw in "for free" has a direct line to Moe's Towing Company.

3. The booster cables are not in the trunk but are permanently soldered to the battery.

4. The hood has been equipped with a push-button device for quick and easy opening.

5. The "Purchased From" sticker at the bottom of the rear license plate has been removed.

6. You get a "Good Luck" card from the previous owner.

7. As you drive up to a service station for gas, the mechanic opens the big door and waves you in.

8. When you leave for work the next morning, you notice a tow truck parked about a block from your driveway. As you go by, it silently falls in behind you.

9. The little "Service Engine" warning signal in the dashboard comes on and reads "Me Again."

NOT A MECHANIC

Q. When is a mechanic not a mechanic?

A. When he turns into an alley.

COOKS DRIVE WHAT?

Q. What kind of cars do cooks drive?

A. Chef-rolets.

IT FLIES?

Q. What has four wheels and flies?

A. A garbage truck.

GENIUS

Q. Did you hear about the genius who couldn't work out how to fasten his seatbelt?

A. Then it clicked.

ALL RIGHT NOW

Q. Did you hear about the guy who lost his left arm and leg in a car crash?

A. He's all right now.

(adapted from www.gemmadorset.com)

OINK!

Q. Why are pigs bad drivers?

A. They hog the road!

SHARP SENIOR

Q. Why did the 80-year-old fellow install a wood stove in his Model A Ford?

A. He wanted to make it a hot rod!

NOT G-A-S-O-L-I-N-E

Q. What has 10 letters and starts with G-A-S?

A. Automobile.

The previous eight question-and-answers jokes adapted from https://thoughtcatalog.com/january-nelson/2018/07/car-puns/

JOY

Q: What makes a car happiest?

A: Joy riding!

OLD TIRES

Q: What would you do if your car's tires got bald?

A: Re-tire them!

WICKED DRIVER

Q: Do you yield when a blind pedestrian is crossing the road?

A: What for? He can't see the license plate!

THE REMAINDER OF THIS CHAPTER IS PRIMARILY
FOR EDITORS OF CAR CLUB MAGAZINES.

LETTERS TO THE EDITOR NEVER ANSWERED

Dear Editor;

I agree with many of your readers' letters. However, I disagree with the others. Please follow THEIR suggestions! - I. M. Equivocal

Dear Editor:

I was very disappointed that *HOT CARS* did not print my recent letter to the editor (which I may have forgotten to write). I am disgusted by this omission. Cancel my subscription (which I am probably late in reviewing). – I. M. Oblivious

SPELL CHEQUER FOUR CAR YOKES

My computer have a spelling chequer four car yokes. It came with my pea sea. It plainly marques four my revue mistakes eye kin knot sea. Eye strike a key and type a word and weight four it two say weather eye am wrong oar write. It shoes me strait a weigh. As soon as a mist ache is maid it honks bee fore two long. And eye can put the error about the car rite. It's rare lea every wrong. Eye have run this paragraph threw it. I am shore your pleased two no. Its letter is perfect awl the weigh. My chequer tolled me sew. *(P.S. This joke should make it all the way through your spell checker with no corrections!)*

(adapted from www.sparkpeople.com; and www.nantyglo.com)

35 RULES FOR WRITERS AND EDITORS

I, Paul Placek, have edited CRUISER NEWS for our local car club the Kent Island Cruisers for nine years, and FoMoCo Times for the Crown Victoria Association for 13 years—total 22 years! I have found myself to be a slave to these rules:

"1. Verbs HAS to agree with their subjects. Cars is pretty.

2. Prepositions are not words to end sentences with.

3. And don't start a sentence with a conjunction. And don't start a paragraph that way either!

4. It is wrong to ever split an infinitive.

5. Avoid clichés like the plague. The car was fast as a lightning bolt.

6. Also, always avoid annoying alliteration.

7. Be more or less specific. Probably, anyways...

8. Parenthetical remarks (however relevant) are (usually) unnecessary. Read on (and enjoy).

9. Also too, never, ever use repetitive redundancies.

10. No sentence fragments. Ever.

11. Contractions aren't necessary and should not never be used.

12. Foreign words and phrases are not apropos. Example: use "aficionado" instead of "enthusiast".

13. Do not be redundant; do not use more words than necessary; it's extremely highly superfluous.

14. One should NEVER generalize. It ALWAYS ruins the article.

15. Comparisons are as bad as clichés. They will leave you as cold as ice.

16. Don't use no double negatives, not never!

17. Eschew ampersands & abbreviations, etc. We & they must avoid them.

18. One-word sentences? Eliminate! Terminate! Exterminate!

19. Analogies in writing are like feathers on a snake. Like greased lightning on a dragstrip.

20. The passive voice is to be ignored. However, this joke book will have been an all-time classic.

21. Eliminate commas, that are, not necessary.

22. Parenthetical words (however) should, usually, be enclosed in commas. We went bonkers (almost) organizing 1,000 jokes.

23. Never use a big word when a diminutive one would suffice.

24. Kill all exclamation points!!!

25. Use words correctly, irregardless of how others use them.

26. Understatement is always the absolute best way to put forth earth-shaking and mind-altering ideas.

27. Use the apostrophe in its' proper place and omit it when its' not needed. Its' not proper.

28. Eliminate quotations. As Ralph Waldo Emerson said, "I hate quotations. Tell me what you know."

29. If you've heard it once, you've heard it a thousand times: Resist hyperbole. Not one writer in a million can use it correctly. Everyone agrees with me.

30. Puns are for children, not groan readers.

31. Go around the barn at high noon to avoid colloquialisms. And don't go there on a dark and stormy night.

32. Even IF a mixed metaphor sings, it should be derailed.

33. Who needs rhetorical questions? Do I?

34. Exaggeration is a billion times worse than understatement.

35. Proofread carefully to see if you any words out."

(adapted from www.ozjokes.com; www.freelancewritinggigs.com; and www.writersstackexchange.com)

With all of these rules which I had to follow, it is a miracle that you ever got this joke book to read. – Paul Placek

THE TYPO

The typographical error

Is a slippery thing and sly,

Till the forms are off the presses

It is strange how still it keeps;

It shrinks down in a corner

And it never stirs or peeps—

The typographical error

Is too small for human eye,

'Till the ink is on the paper...

Then it grows to mountain size.

The boss, he stars with horror,

Then grabs his hair and groans;

The copy reader drops his head

Upon his hands and moans.

The remainder of the issue

 May be clean as clean can be.

But the typographical error

Is the olny things you see.

 ----Author unknown.

GOOD GRAMMAR, GOOD TASTE

Dear Editor: "Just a comment on your editorial skills. If you're the one putting the quotation marks inside the periods and the commas and the semi-colons, it's almost always incorrect that way (unless you're in England—but we're not). If you don't believe me, check "grammar.com" or the website on the enclosed sheet. Also dollar figures do not require a decimal point and two zeros. Only when it is not an even dollar amount do you use decimals, e.g., $2.75, etc. Yes, I was a secretary from 1961 until 2003." Vivian B., ND.

EDITOR'S REPLY: Dear Vivian: "As I always's say: "Each to his own". We doo appreciate you're paying you're doos promptly each annual year. If wee every hav an opining for a proofe reeder, wee wil contac yoo."

Editor-- Paul Placek

SMART EDITOR?

Travis, the Esteemed Editor of FoMoCo Times, took a powerboat into the Chesapeake Bay. A huge storm came up and he was in danger of sinking. So he called 911 and asked for the marine police. The police asked: "What is your position. Repeat! What is your position?" His chest swelled with pride: "My position? Why, I'm the Editor of the FoMoCo Times in the Crown Victoria Association!"

AUTHOR'S DILEMMA

Paul Placek (author of this joke book) to wife: "Do you think I should put more fire into my jokes?" Rebecca Placek (wife): "No, you should put more jokes in the fire." Paul: "So, you don't like my jokes?" Rebecca: "Some of them are OK. I threw some into the fireplace and the fire roared."

FINAL ADVICE FROM THE AUTHOR

If you have enjoyed this book of jokes for car lovers, well, you make sure you drive safely when you next drive your car. But if you *haven't* enjoyed this book, well, who am I to tell you how to drive?

IF YOU FIND MISTAKES...

If you find mistakes about cars in this joke book, please consider that they are there for a purpose. We try to publish something for everyone, and some people are always looking for mistakes!